ROCK-SOLId
FAMILIES

ROCK-SOLID FAMILIES

TRANSFORMING AN ORDINARY HOME INTO A FORTRESS OF FAITH

JANELL RARDON

Living Ink Books
An Imprint of AMG Publishers

ISBN 987-089957-036-5

First printing—September 2007
Cover designed by ImageWright,Inc., Chattanooga, Tennessee
Interior design and typesetting by Reider Publishing Services,
    West Hollywood, California
Edited and Proofread by Rich Cairnes, Dan Penwell, Sharon Neal,
    and Rick Steele

Printed in the United States of America
13 12 11 10 09 08 07–V– 8 7 6 5 4 3 2 1

To my rock-solid husband and best friend, Rob.
Twenty-three years ago, you told me
you would "lasso the moon" for me.
And, you did.
We truly have a wonderful life.

To my rock-solid children,
Candace, Brooke, and Grant.
You are the absolute joy of my life.
You are the reason I was born.
I love you more than you will ever know.

To my rock-solid retriever, Abraham.
Thank you for barking me away from the computer.
Because of you—I saw the sunshine at least once a day.

CONTENTS

ACKNOWLEDGMENTS

It has been said, "The journey of a thousand miles begins with a single step." *Rock-Solid Families'* first step was a simple invitation by my friend, Cherrie Moore, to write a monthly column for her regional magazine, *The Bayith Educator*. These practical articles then became the "Family Foundations" section of *The Virginia Homeschool Manual* published by my friends at HEAV—*The Home Educator's Association of Virginia*. You gave voice to my passion for the institute of family and I'm deeply grateful for the opportunity.

Rock-Solid Families would not have taken its next step without Dan Penwell, my editor, whose keen eyes and sharp mind have molded this manuscript and raised my standard of excellence in writing. Because of you, I will never again be referred to as "a first-time author."

Thank you to Rich Cairnes, a perceptive, tremendous editor and to Sharon Neal for a fabulous job of proofreading.

And I so appreciate the creative individuals at AMG Publishers: Dale Anderson, Joe Suter, Trevor Overcash, Rick Steele, Warren Baker, Karen Moreland, Gin Chasten, Amanda Donahoe, and Donna Coker. I owe you a big batch of my colossal chocolate chip cookies.

A special word of appreciation to Nancy Jernigan, my amazing literary agent. Your invitation to be part of *Hidden Value Group* took me by total surprise. Within minutes of our meeting, I knew God had a special plan. We might be three thousand miles apart physically, but spiritually, I feel you are right next door. Thank you for walking beside me on this challenging journey.

What would a journey be without family and friends?

Mom, thank you for being a faithful woman. One of my best childhood memories is nestling next to you in church. It was here that my sensitivity to spiritual matters was birthed as I realized there was a God in control of the universe.

Thank you Sandy and Teresa—your rock-solid friendships are my spiritual holdfast.

I so appreciate you, Pastor Ruffin Alphin. Week after week, you incite me to "follow hard after God." And thank you to the rest of my family at WRPC for your love and support.

Thank you to my special friends at Denbigh Baptist Christian School.

Love and appreciation to my wise, patient husband, Rob, and our three children—Candace, Brooke, and Grant. Thank you for bringing me so much joy. You have been the source and inspiration for this book. *My cup runneth over.*

Ancora Imparo
("I am still learning.")

INTRODUCTION
Raising a Strong Family Is a *Now* Job!

Looking into the eyes of a child always gives me confidence that the world is a great place to be. Through their eyes, I begin to wonder again: *Why is the sky blue? Why do leaves change colors in the fall? Why do caterpillars turn into butterflies? Why does a ladybug have black spots? Why do bees sting? Who is God? Where is heaven?*

Children are curious about everything. Their entire world is a canvas of opportunity, delight, and adventure. Their infinite joy in the simple things and their voracious appetite to learn are a wake-up call to those of us who have perhaps become dulled by the monotonous tones of daily life.

Sometimes, as parents, we are annoyed by the constant barrage of questions, but we must remember that asking questions is a golden opportunity for stimulating conversation that can ultimately develop great thinkers. This natural curiosity is the gateway to true education, scholarship, and life-changing truths. A wise parent will take a very deep breath after the hundredth question of the day and answer one last question before tucking a child into bed.

At a seminar I was attending, the question was posed, "What do you pound the table over?" A simple question with serious overtones. The speaker wanted us to examine our passion, our heart, our mission. Driving home, I once again thought about the question and concluded two things:

1. I'd pound the table in my desire to help others develop a personal relationship with Jesus Christ—a life of spirituality, holiness, and righteousness.
2. I'd pound the table in my desire to help families develop strong, stable, and spiritually enabled homes—places where children can be masterfully crafted into servants and witnesses for Christ.

The forces of evil are attacking the institution of the family in full force. The home is at a crossroads according to a recent survey, "The Top Ten Issues Facing Families:

> They will decide whether or not to sustain a social institution that has been around for thousands of years and has made possible such practices as the care of children and respect for women. On one side are destructive forces of pornography, the anonymity of the Internet, alcohol, abuse, an unattainable ideal of success, the idols of youth and beauty, normalization of adultery, unsustainable consumerism, and a faltering social code of dignity and propriety. On the other side is the church—armed with the promise of redemption in Christ. It is striving to show mercy and grace to individuals negatively impacted . . . as instigators or victims . . . when behaviors fall outside of God's plan for a supportive, unified family. In a survey of ministry leaders from a wide range of denominations from America and beyond, the seventh most pressing issue facing the church is the multitude of problems stemming from the dissolution of the institution of marriage and the ever-decreasing nucleus of the traditional family.[1]

The home must become the fortress of faith as it fortifies the family. Webster's dictionary defines *fortify* as:

1. To surround with a wall, ditch, palisades, or other works, with a view to defend against the attacks of an enemy.

2. To strengthen against any attack.
3. To confirm; to add strength and firmness to.
4. To furnish with strength or means of resisting force, violence, or assault.[2]

Key words in those definitions are *surround, strengthen, confirm, add,* and *furnish*—all verbs that imply action and hard work on our part. Good, old-fashioned, roll-up-your-sleeves-and-get-down-to-it hard work. Maintaining a marvelous marriage is not easy. Raising a family by training our children to follow after God is tough work. But please—*please*—know this! *God gives us the energy to do what he has called us to do.*

On several occasions I have had the privilege of listening to author and missionary, Elisabeth Elliot. Countless times she referenced Philip E. Howard, her wise father. He advised her that

> every parent who dares to take upon himself the responsibility of calling a human life into being, who places himself in God's hands as the instrument of divine creative power, assumes a trust which should exclude every form of selfishness. Beyond the right of being well born, every child has the right to the best training his parent can give. He has the right to the personal care of both father and mother, a care which can never be delegated to others without serious loss to both parent and child. It is a part of holy intimacy . . .

When I was a little girl, someone gave me a shoot from a mimosa tree. I planted this tender shoot with such loving care, right in the front yard of my family's little house. I wanted it to grow so bad it hurt. I watched it every day. I watered it. I fertilized it. I'm sure I even prayed to God to help it grow. Somehow, it made me feel connected to God—to something bigger than myself. Then one day a terrible storm came. I remember running outside with a black garbage bag, covering and securing it so it could survive the tempestuous storm. *Oh, God, please protect my little mimosa*. After the storm passed, I held my breath and checked to see how it was doing. A little tattered, but all was well. Years passed and my mimosa grew tall. Its outstretched branches and pink blossoms swayed in the wind as if they were worshipping God.

My mimosa tree taught me the vital elements of nurture: time, tenderness, love, protection, proper nutrients, and—most importantly—prayer. I can't pass by a mimosa tree today without smiling and remembering those elements.

My mother-in-law, Carolyn, a wise woman, took me aside once and told me, "Janell, do something no one else can do. Remember that God has entrusted you with a wonderful family, and parenting is a sacred trust between you and God." A trust. A *sacred* trust. Strong words, but very, very true. Every child is deserving of the best training parents can give.

So I made a commitment to give mothering my all. I asked questions. Many questions. I studied, prayed, sought counsel, and listened to others wiser than myself. I made a habit of talking to young adults and strong families about their child-rearing experiences and practices. On a daily basis, I made hard decisions about my commitments outside the home. As a parent, I was constantly asking questions and making adjustments to allow myself more time and more energy for nurturing my children and creating a rock-solid home.

One persistent truth continually ignites my passion—I can't do this job over again. Other opportunities will come and go, but raising a strong family is a *now* job. Right now. I can't put it off until tomorrow. I can't wake up today and ask for the day off, call in sick, decide I want to quit—not without serious consequences to my children.

When I stand before God, I will be held accountable. And on that day, I long to hear him say, "Well done! Good job!" (see Matthew 25:21).

May I repeat: Raising a strong family is hard work. No doubt about it. I liken it to a marathon. An emotional, spiritual, physical, and mental marathon from sunrise to sunset. But, at the end of this marathon is the finish line—and the prize of a great family. I've done many, many things in my life and accomplished a great deal, but nothing—absolutely nothing—compares to the great joy I have felt in watching my children mature into great adults.

One Sunday morning, I felt a gentle touch on my shoulder. "Janell, who are those three beautiful adults standing next to you?" whispered Nancy. I turned my head and saw a precious young mother with tears in her eyes.

"They are mine. Isn't it amazing?" Holding back tears of my own, I felt so deeply blessed, richly content.

God, you are so good. Look what you have done. Here beside me is my prize. What a great family you have given me. You really were listening to that little girl peering out her window. You answered that prayer I cried out so many years ago. Thank you, God. Thank you so much.

Never in a million years could I have imagined the elation motherhood would bring to me. Where are the trophies of my youth? Gathering dust in my attic. On the contrary, the trophies of my present are gathering memories in my heart. I can honestly say I was born to mother my three children. If I die today, I know with a certainty that I have done my best to fulfill my eternal mission.

The tragedy of September 11, 2001, was a clarion call to all of us. There is no way to avoid the sobering truth that life is short, life is fragile, and life is a gift. While celebrating our twenty-second wedding anniversary in Scotland, news of other terrorist threats spread rapidly. News anchors reported that plans had been set in motion to bomb transatlantic flights leaving the United Kingdom.

"Those bombs were meant for us," I soberly remarked.

"That's right, but the plans have been stalled," my husband assured me. Quicker than lightning, I found an Internet café and sent an email to our three children. With a six-hour time difference, I knew they would wake up to this message in their inbox.

"Pray. Pray hard," I wrote. "We are not sure when the airports will resume normal flight schedules. Pray we get out of Scotland—safely."

Unsure of what lay ahead, I prayed fervently. Late that night, my husband and I huddled in a red Scottish phone booth, inserted countless coins, and assured our three children that God would be faithful. Right there, separated by the Atlantic Ocean, we prayed as a family—"Lord, you are a strong tower. We run to you. You are our ever-present help in times of trouble."

Two days later, after a long delay, countless security checks, and heightened awareness of the presence of evil in the world, we embarked on our transatlantic flight from Scotland to America. The gravity of the situation weighed heavily on each member of our little family, knowing that in the event something did happen, each would assume a great deal of responsibility. But it's in times like these that the character of a family is revealed.

Twenty-two years earlier, my husband and I had moved into an ordinary home. But, after years of trials and tests, there is nothing ordinary about our family. Our ordinary home became a fortress of faith against the tyranny of evil that exists in this world.

As I write this, "evil" walked into West Ambler Johnson Dormitory and Norris Hall on the campus of Virginia Tech University in Blacksburg, Virginia, and took the lives of thirty-two students and faculty members. That horrific day, April 16, 2007, will be remembered for the deadliest mass shooting in American history. Once again, an unfathomable tragedy has stunned our nation.

The funeral of one victim, Nicole White, was held at a church in my community. Nicole, a twenty-year-old junior, thought she was just going to class. Friends tell me that Nicole's parents find solace and rest in the fact that Nicole knew Jesus Christ. Seeing a rock-solid family stand firm through this tragedy reminds me that homes must be fortresses of faith in this unpredictable world.

In her well-written book, *Choices*, Mary Farrar writes as follows,

> Amazing what a crisis will reveal about the hidden character of a nation—or an individual. Values surface quickly in the middle of a crisis, don't they? Whether we realize it or not, the critical choices we make in times of crisis can become matters of life and death. I submit to you there is nothing in this world more important than our homes, our marriages, and our children. Nothing. There is not one ministry or job or accomplishment or calling that is more important . . . The family is not just an arm or a finger. It is the very heart. And everyone knows if you have a bad heart, you are in serious trouble.[3]

As you read *Rock-Solid Famlies*, you will find it's divided into twelve sections called "Foundation Stones." It is my hope that these twelve Foundation Stones will guide you and your family exactly where you want to go. It may be a rough journey at times, but one thing is certain: God is an ever-present help to each of us (see Psalm 46:1). I certainly don't claim to have all the answers, but I know the One who does. Let me serve as your guide—one called to help you build a strong family, a fortress of faith.

Years ago, I discovered a powerful account in Judges 9:50–55. It tells of a woman locked away in a strong tower in the middle of a city called Thebez. When the news that Abimelech, a Philistine ruler and enemy of Israel, and his army were en route to destroy the city, all the inhabitants of Thebez raced to the tower for safety. Locking the door behind them, they all headed to the roof. As Abimelech came to the entrance to set the tower on fire, the woman in focus dropped a millstone on him, crushing his head. Abimelech, not yet dead, commanded his armor bearer to slay him so it wouldn't be said of him that he died at the hand of a woman.

Several significant thoughts emerged in my heart after meditating upon this passage:

- Who was this brave woman?
- What gave her the physical strength and spiritual fortitude to stand against Abimelech? How on earth did she pick up the heavy millstone?
- Why did *she* drop the millstone? Why not a man? Or a child? Scholars suggest it was to further crush Abimelech's pride—to be killed by the hand of a woman would have been a disgrace.
- What on earth led her to take such action? Did she have children she was protecting? Or perhaps word had spread of Abimelech's army killing more than one thousand people in the nearby tower of Shechem (Judges 9:49).

I concluded by challenging myself, "Shouldn't I be as vehement against the prevailing evil confronting my home, family, and community?"

At the end of each chapter in this book is an activity section called "Time in the Tower." The woman of Thebez faced one of the greatest challenges of her life in that tower. Something tells me her entire life and family flashed before her eyes. With adrenaline surging through her body and no time to think, I can hear her scream, "Now, right now! Move out of my way! We have to stop him before he destroys everything!"

She knew all about the power of *now*. A little word with great big ramifications. Remember, building a strong family is a *now* job—and that means *right now.*

Time in the Tower

Raising a Family Is a *Now* Job!

1. Think about the word *now*. Three little letters. Read through the following Scripture passages. See the emphasis on living in the now. If you have access to the Internet, use www.biblegateway.com to search the different versions available.

I love reading the Scriptures in *The Message* version—Eugene Peterson has done an incredible job of making them simple and practical.

- 2 Corinthians 6:1–3. See the emphasis on "now"—"now is the day."
- Matthew 6:25–34. What is Jesus saying in verse 34?
- Genesis 24:12. Take to heart Abraham's chief servant's prayer: "Then he prayed, 'O Lord, God of my master Abraham, give me success today, and show kindness to my master Abraham.' "

2. "Give me success today." What do you need the Lord to give you success in *today*? Take the time to think about this. Here, at the onset of your journey to transform an ordinary home into a fortress of faith, write a letter to God about what you desire for your family, then answer: What do I want my family to look like a year from now? Five years from now? Okay—twenty years from now? (Before you know it, it will *be* twenty years from now.)

Notes

1. Lifeway Resources, "Top Ten Issues Facing Today's Church: #7 Marriage." http://www.lifeway.com/lwc/rd_article_content/0,2815,A %253D159483%2526X%253D1%2526M%253D200812,00.thml (accessed 16 December 2006).

2. Noah Webster, *An American Dictionary of the English Language* (New York: S. Converse, 1828). Facsimile first edition (Chesapeake, VA: Foundation for American Christian Education, 1967 and all subsequent editions).

3. Mary Farrar, *Choices: For Women Who Long to Discover Life's Best* (Colorado Springs: Multnomah, 1994), 18.

VISION
The Fire of Focus

"The greatest tragedy in life is not death, but life without reason. It is dangerous to be alive and not know why you were given life. The deepest craving of the human spirit is to find a sense of significance and relevance. The search for relevance in life is the ultimate pursuit of man. Conscious or unconscious, admitted or unadmitted, this internal passion is what motivates and drives every human being, either directly or indirectly. It directs his decisions, controls his behavior and dictates his responses to his environment."[1]

Author and researcher George Barna, in *The Power of Vision*, defines *vision* as "a picture held in your mind's eye of the way things could or should be in the days ahead. It is not somebody else's view of the future, but one that uniquely belongs to you."[2] The key here is that God's plan for your family is tailor-made—fitted perfectly—unlike anyone else's. Don't compete. Don't compare (only to raise your own standard or when in need of help). Don't stray from the path you've chosen.

When I was a young girl, my soul yearned for answers. Somewhere deep in my little girl heart, I suspected my life wasn't "normal." I wondered:

Did every little girl pray for her daddy to stop drinking?

Did every little girl pray her mommy and daddy would stay together?

Did every little girl cry herself to sleep, full of worry and despair? Somehow, I didn't think so.

My family of origin today would be labeled "dysfunctional" because my father was an alcoholic. This type of home environment infuses a sense of instability and insecurity.

Will Daddy come home drunk or sober?

Will he come home at all? Will he show up at my school drunk and embarrass me?

What will my friends think?

Why won't he stop drinking?

But somewhere underneath all the questions was a dream, a vision. God, in his infinite mercy, looked down from heaven and whispered a dream into the depths of my heart . . . the dream of a normal family. He knew that one day this little girl would grow up, beat the odds of becoming another statistic, and champion the cause of family. Pastor and author Andy Stanley puts it this way:

> There is always a moral element to vision. Vision carries with it a sense of conviction. Anyone with a vision will tell you this is not merely something that *could* be done. This is something that *should* be done. This is something that *must* happen. It is the element that catapults men and women out of the realm of passive concern and into action. It is the moral element that gives the vision a sense of urgency. Vision is a preferred future. A destination. Vision always stands in contrast to the world as it is. Vision demands change. It implies movement. But a vision requires someone to champion the cause.[3]

I would be that someone! Why does a little girl sense that she wants a *normal* family—one where Daddy doesn't drink? Because God, in his infinite mercy and compassion, pulled back the curtains of my reality and gave me a glimpse into the supernatural. He filled my heart with amazing hope. He helped me believe in the impossible. And then, years later, he placed it within me to champion the cause.

I stand amazed that Almighty God, sitting on the throne of heaven, heard the cries of my heart and saw the tears fall upon my face so many years ago. I remember those tears as if they were cried yesterday. Why? Because they were an offering. A prayer. A silent plea. They were the beginning of years of intercession on behalf of my father and my family. Intercession and tears often go hand in hand, as do weeping and intense emotion. Somehow, I envision the woman of Thebez weeping while interceding by casting down her millstone.

David, the psalmist, understood the power of this process: "You've kept track of my every toss and turn through the sleepless nights, Each tear entered in your ledger, each ache written in your book" (Psalm 56:8, MSG). Noted Bible commentator Matthew Henry offers, "God has a bottle and a book for his people's tears, both the tears for their sins, and those for their afflictions. He observes them with tender concern." Isn't it comforting to know that God catches our tears? That he writes down in his book each tear? After twenty-two years of parenting, I am sure I have a complete library!

But, the best news of all is that these tears do not remain tears. No, they are transformed into joy. Psalm 126:5 records, "Those who sow in tears will reap with songs of joy." Somewhere in your future, God will transform the tears you have cried into a delightful song of

> "Weeping may remain for a night, but rejoicing comes in the morning."
> (Psalm 30:5)

joy! Right now, you may be in the midst of a season of weeping. Don't resist the work God is doing. Your desires for your family are his desires. He wants to make your family great. Whatever obstacles are standing in the way, cry out to him to remove them. One by one. And as you face these obstacles, with God by your side, face the future with great anticipation.

Writing Your Family Mission Statement

As I try to understand my life now, while looking backward, I can trace the hand of God gently holding my tender heart and see how he was and is at work. He was present at my birth, walked me through some difficult places in my childhood, awakened me spiritually during my latter college years, and every day since has given me an even greater passion for the covenant of family. He gave me a vision and I have never let go of it.

Vision has a plan. Vision has a future in mind. Vision awaits activity. First and foremost, as parents, it is essential that we have such vision for our own families. We begin by drafting a family mission statement. Businesses spend countless hours and dollars on developing their business plans.

> "Faith trusts in advance what will only make sense in reverse."[4]

They even hire marketing experts who chisel away until they are left with a rock-solid one-line slogan or motto that all the world will recite over and over again. You know them: *Just Do It! Have It Your Way! It's the Real Thing!*

Why shouldn't parents do the same thing? Habakkuk 2:2 says, "Write down the revelation and make it plain on tablets so that a herald may run with it." Five ingredients are essential for crafting a rock-solid, one-line family mission statement:

1. *Make Jesus Christ the focal point.* As a Christian family, your primary purpose is to glorify God. He is the axis upon which your family will rotate.

2. *Make it short and sweet.* A rock-solid one-liner is just that. One line. No longer.

3. *Make it crystal clear.* Use your own words. Make certain every member of the family, from the youngest to the oldest, can understand it and easily recite it.

4. *Make it reasonable.* One of the wisest pieces of advice I have ever received was to set reasonable goals. Now obviously, there is a time to dream big, but in crafting your family mission statement, be reasonable. Setting unreasonable goals will result in a sense of failure when they are not met. Some examples of reasonable mission statements:

   "The _____ family will follow hard after God."
   "The _____ family will uphold God's Word."
   "The _____ family loves truth."
   "The _____ family builds one another up in holy love."

   Some unreasonable mission statements might be:

   "The _____ family will never lie."
   "The _____ family will always get along."
   "The _____ family will help every person in the world."
   "The _____ family will never miss a church meeting."
   "The _____ family will never yell."

5. *Make it reflect the gifts and talents of each family member.* My friends Lou and Teresa are following in the footsteps of Gaius (see Romans 16:23)—they practice hospitality (see Romans 12:13) with the utmost distinction. My older daughter and I recently spent a couple of days with them and left feeling immensely blessed. Isn't that how Paul felt after leaving Gaius?

> "Without purpose, life is an experiment or a haphazard journey that results in frustration, disappointment or failure. Without purpose, life is subjective, or it is a trial and error game that is ruled by environmental influences and the circumstances of the moment. Likewise, in the absence of purpose, time has no meaning, energy has no reason and life has no precision."[5]

The next three sections will help you get started in thinking about what you want your family mission statement to say.

Vision and Values

Ask yourself:

- Who are we?
- What does our family stand for?
- What do we believe?
- What values, activities, and/or causes are important to us? *Church? Athletics? Academics? Work? Politics? Homeschooling? Travel? Community service?*
- Are we givers? Philanthropists? Supporters of missions? ("God loves a cheerful giver" (2 Corinthians 9:7).)
- What is our conviction concerning education? *Public school? Private school? Homeschool? College-bound? Apprenticeships?*

During my first pregnancy, someone recommended reading Edith Schaeffer's *What Is a Family?* Edith's words deeply affected me. She set the course for my parenting by gently encouraging me to see my family in thirty to forty years . . . at our first family reunion. I knew what I wanted to see—my husband and me still together after all that time, a family that shared a strong faith in God, grandchildren being raised in spiritually healthy homes filled with laughter, joy, and lots of love. And, here I am, some twenty-one years later, a little "weary in well doing" (Galatians 6:9, KJV), but overwhelmed at the goodness of God, who fulfills the desires of our hearts.

> "A personal mission statement acts as both a harness and a sword, harnessing you to what is true about your life, and cutting away all that is false."[6]

Purpose and Passion

Does your family have a particular interest or shared passion? If so, this should be incorporated into your mission statement. Coming from a military family, I know firsthand that the whole family is affected each time a promotion comes, orders are received, or the parent is deployed. This family's purpose would definitely harness certain opportunities and require incredible grace, focus, and determination to remain united.

Perhaps you own a family business, as we do. This requires certain decisions, constant maintenance, and flexibility. The first five years of our marriage, my husband was building a business. Never in a million years could we have imagined the great harvest that would come from those difficult years of sacrifice. But because we were in sync with our vision, we pressed on toward our goal. We knew short-term sacrifice would produce long-term benefits for our family.

Is someone in your family in the ministry full-time? Pastor? Worship leader? Bible teacher? Lay minister? If so, this will definitely affect family dynamics.

Are there any physical limitations in your family? Is someone handicapped? Physically or emotionally challenged? While that might limit your family in some ways, it might also open up opportunities for ministry.

Discipline and Determination

I am constantly repeating my mothering mission statement to myself:

TRAIN MY CHILDREN—SPIRIT, SOUL, AND BODY—FOR THEIR FUTURE STATIONS IN LIFE.

And our family mission statement:

STAND STRONG, TRUE, AND ABLE AS A FAMILY OF FAITH.

Regardless of the opportunities that unfold before us, we must be disciplined and put blinders on to remain focused on family mission. Does this job opportunity support what we desire to have as a family? Do these activities for the children allow us to be the family we feel called to be?

Several summers ago, my son, Grant, fifteen at the time, was invited to be a starting varsity soccer player on a well-respected private-school team. This offer couldn't have come at a more difficult time. Our family was in the midst of moving from the country into the city—and it was August. School was to start in ten days.

To make a long story short, we prayed and prayed and decided this was God's will for Grant and the rest of our family. We made a corporate decision based on our family's mission. We weighed all the options, listed the pros and cons, and prayed. There was nothing profound about the process—we merely assessed the options, remembered our family's purpose, listened to the inner nudging of the Holy Spirit, and made a decision.

The Three Lenses

Through the years, I've noticed there are three lenses through which we see life: focused, distracted, and blurred.

Mr. Miyagi, in the 1984 blockbuster film *The Karate Kid*, tried to teach his young student, Daniel Russo, the fire of a focused life. "Focus, Daniel-san, focus." With two hands framing Daniel's face, he repeated this command over and over.

"We make sacred pact," Mr. Miyagi said. "I promise teach karate to you, you promise learn. I say, you do. No questions."

I could almost sense God placing his hands around my face saying, "Focus, Janell-san, focus. We make sacred pact. I promise guide you, you promise follow. I say, you do. No questions."

That is why wise King Solomon instructed us in Proverbs 4:25–27, "Let your eyes look straight ahead, fix your gaze directly before you. Make level paths for your feet and take only ways that are firm. Do not swerve to the right or the left; keep your foot from evil." A fixed gaze is the opposite of the "lust of [one's] eye" (1 John 2:16), which is always looking to and fro for something more appealing, more appetizing, and more alluring.

Matthew Henry urges, "We need to make a covenant with our eyes. Let the eye be fixed [*focused*] and not wandering [*distracted*]; let it not rove everything that presents itself, for then it will be diverted from good and ensnared in evil."[7] Don't let Henry's Old English baffle you. When he states, "Let it not rove everything that presents itself," he means: *there will be countless opportunities that cross your path. Many of them will be very, very good. Good is usually very tempting, indeed. Good loves to sneak in the door right before Best. But stay focused. Don't let Good in the door—Best will be knocking soon.*

Years ago, Distraction and I had a knockdown, drag-out fight. She can be a tough opponent. In just one second, she can extinguish the fire of focus. I wrote in my journal,

> I am looking in the mirror this Sunday morning and seeing a reflection that needs altering. Life . . . my biggest challenge. I haven't written in months. How does a writer forego the beneficial medicine of recording her struggles and triumphs

in the heart of her journal? How does this happen? Slowly. I have once again found myself trapped and entangled in the clutches of Distraction. My home business has pervaded my life, becoming a demanding entity—distracting and drawing my attention aside from the path of marriage and family. Isn't this the constant battle of my life? I enjoy creative work, but of late I do not enjoy being out until eleven o'clock at night—driving home weak, fatigued, pained, and unprepared for the homeschooling that needs to be the priority. I know this isn't right. Help me, Lord, to find the fire of focus.

Herein lies the secret:

> When we fix our eyes on Jesus, the Eternal One,
> our souls are hushed,
> our hearts are quieted,
> our minds are focused,
> and our lives are contented.

Think back with me for a minute. Mr. Miyagi knew exactly what Daniel needed. As Daniel's wise mentor, Mr. Miyagi tried to impress on his student that a distracted mind would be his downfall. Daniel was running a hundred miles per hour, thinking way too much and trying to do things his way. Daniel had become discontented with Mr. Miyagi, but his discontent grew out of his own distraction. His mind was crowded and confused by all the voices calling him in different directions. Finally, after many hard knocks, Daniel finally acquiesced to his wise mentor. Listen to another wise man and what he had to say about the fruit of focus—contentment:

> I am not saying this because I am in need, for I have learned to be content whatever the circumstances. I know what it is to be in need, and I know what it is to have plenty. I have

learned the secret of being content in any and every situation, whether well fed or hungry, whether living in plenty or in want. I can do everything through him who gives me strength. (Philippians 4:11–13)

Paul tells us twice that he has learned the secret of being content. After pondering this, I asked myself, "Why the big secret? If being content is so important, why would it be such a secret?" Could the answer to this question be found in Deuteronomy 29:29? "The secret things belong to the LORD our God, but the things revealed belong to us and to our children forever, that we may follow all the words of this law."

After numerous close encounters with death, "Paul was content to have Christ—period. That is possible only for the Christian who knows the meaning of 'the surpassing greatness of knowing Christ Jesus my Lord' and in that light counts other things to be 'rubbish' by comparison (Philippians 3:8)."[8] Scottish theologian Sinclair Ferguson continues, "These words teach us that it is possible, by the grace of God, to be content, even in a world like this where we face trial, difficulty and deprivation. They are also words of experience, indicating that the contentment Paul describes is not to be confused with our natural temperament. Spiritual contentment needs to be learned, and usually is so through hard or testing experiences."[9]

Years ago, my doctor issued a very unusual prescription. He wanted me to take six months off from leadership responsibilities.

"Did you say six months?" I asked.

"Yes, that's right," he said. "I'm really concerned. I know the signs—and you have all of them. You won't make it another six months if you don't stop being responsible for the world. I want you to take care of your little girl and your home. And, I want you to learn to take care of yourself. Do you know how to take care of yourself? Give yourself permission to rest."

I wanted him to tell me I had a physical problem. Not an emotional one. My thoughts whirled like a pinwheel:

- What are you going to do?
- What will people think?
- What about all the children you teach, and Children's Church? You write the curriculum. What now?
- You are going to be so bored. Stay home? I don't think so.
- What about money? Your extra money? You won't be able to buy anything at all! You will be strapped.

That was a tough day for me. For the first time in my life, someone saw through my facade and gave me permission to take care of myself. Perhaps you know exactly how I felt. Perhaps your circumstances are overwhelming you. Or causing discontent or distraction. Or even frazzling your family? I sense that God has placed you in the midst of these circumstances in order to demonstrate his great love for you and to help you learn spiritual contentment. Stop for a moment and answer the following questions:

- What difficult circumstances are stirring up discontent in your life?
- Are you trying to control the circumstances or are you letting God control them?
- What one thing can you do, right now, to eliminate the distraction(s) that are crowding your mind and causing discontent in your family?
- What one thing can you do to help you focus solely on God and his Word?
- Okay, do it. Take your first step toward contentment.

I'm here to encourage you. If God can help me learn to be spiritually content, he can definitely help you. I testify that I finally learned contentment, that Philippians 4:11–13 contentment, and it is very, very sweet. I will never go back to living a discontented, distracted life.

Jeremiah Burroughs (1599–1646), a member of the Westminster Assembly and an insightful writer, coined the best definition of contentment I've ever read. "Contentment," he writes, "is that sweet inward, quiet, gracious frame of spirit which freely submits to and delights in God's wise and Fatherly disposal in every condition."[10] *In every condition.* Impossible? I'm sure you think it is, but "with God all things are possible" (Matthew 19:26).

Blurred vision is poisonous to a focused life. When something is blurry, it impedes progress. Living on the eastern seaboard, we are familiar with hurricanes and the pounding thunderstorms that accompany them. Driving through them is virtually impossible. Why? Because the torrential downpours blur any hope of driving safely. It is almost mandatory to drive off the road and sit the storm out. Then, and only then, can one continue. As our eyes begin to focus on God, we can be assured that he will lead our families in the right direction, helping us stay on the pathway he has designed. Distraction ceases when we activate the powerful principle of focus, negating the blur. Matthew 6:22–23 states, "The eye is the lamp of the body. If your eyes are good [focused], your whole body will be full of light. But if your eyes are bad [distracted or blurred], your whole body will be full of darkness."

In the "Time in the Tower" section of this chapter, you will draft your family mission statement. Before you begin, imagine God cupping his hands around your face. Gently, he instructs:

"Slow down, __(your name)__, slow down. You are in such a hurry."

"Rest, __(your name)__, rest. I want you to rest for a while."

"Focus, _ (your name)__, focus. I want you to focus."

Time in the Tower

The Fire of Focus

1. Here we go. Standing at the threshold of transformation, spend time pondering and discussing the attributes of your family. Now that you've answered all the questions in this chapter, fill in the bubble chart below with your family's interests, passions, and/or gifts. This makes creating your family mission statement much more manageable.

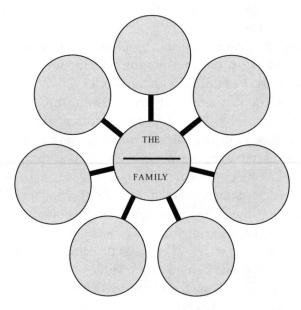

2. Now, right now, you are ready to begin crafting your family's mission statement. Remember the rules: Make Jesus the focal point. Make it short and sweet. Make it crystal clear. Make it reasonable. Make it reflect the giftings and talents of each family member. Use the charts below to write down a rough draft first, then the final draft. When you are done, put it in a visible place where all family members can see it. And, remember Winston Churchill's famous mission statement: "Never, never, never give up!"

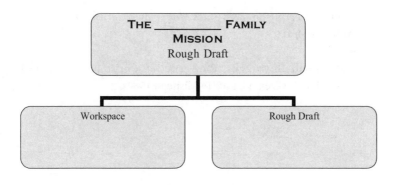

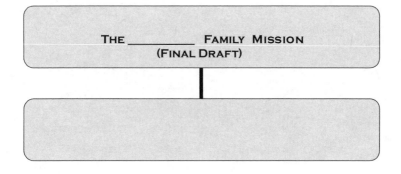

Notes

1. Myles Munroe, *In Pursuit of Purpose* (Shippensburg, PA: Destiny Image, 1992), Preface.

2. George Barna, *The Power of Vision* (Ventura, CA: Regal Books, 1992), 29.

3. Andy Stanley, *Visioneering* (Sisters, OR: Multnomah, 1999), 17–18.

4. Philip Yancey, *Disappointment with God* (Grand Rapids, MI: Zondervan, 1988), 224.

5. Myles Munroe, *In Pursuit of Purpose*, 5–6.

6. Laurie Beth Jones, *The Path: Creating Your Mission Statement*, 3.

7. Christian Classics Ethereal Library, "Matthew Henry's Commentary on the Whole Bible [Volume Index]," http://www.ccel.org/ccel/henry/mhc.i.html (accessed November 12, 2006).

8. Sinclair Ferguson, *Let's Study Philippians* (Carlisle, PA: Banner of Truth, 2005), 109.

9. Ibid.

10. Jeremiah Burroughs, *Rare Jewel of Christian Contentment* (Lafayette, IN: Sovereign Grace Publishers, 1964), 2.

2

FLEXIBILITY
Think Change!

One afternoon my children and I were shopping, when a framed picture caught my eye. In bold print, the words "Think Change!" jumped out at me. I immediately walked over and stood in front of it. *"Think change!"* I repeated to myself. *"Think change!"* Interesting concept. A paradox of sorts, because who likes change? Who actually wants to think about change? I certainly don't. Not *real* change. I don't mind changing purses, changing socks, changing bed linens, changing from winter to spring clothing, but what about changing jobs, changing homes, changing churches, changing families (as is required after a loved one dies or divorces and a remarriage occurs), or changing habits or behavioral patterns? Yes, what about changing habits?

Habits become entrenched and are tenacious when it comes to uprooting them. I would have to agree with the old Chinese proverb, "Habits are cobwebs at first; cables at last."[1] It is easy to develop a habit, but hard to break one. Why is that? Because initiating change, from the inside out, is painstaking work. It involves making a resolution written in stone.

"New ideas stir from every corner. They show up disguised innocently as interruptions, contradictions and embarrassing dilemmas. Beware of total strangers and friends alike who shower you with comfortable sameness, and remain open to those who make you uneasy, for they are the true messengers of the future."[2]

"The bend in the road is not the end of the road unless you refuse to take the turn."[3]

As I meditated on these two little words—*Think change!*—I began learning big lessons about myself and about God. I realized God has been in the business of changing lives since the beginning of time. As written in Romans 12:2, we are to spend our days being transformed—completely changed—by the renewing of our minds. Why? So we will be prepared to meet God face-to-face in eternity. The following quotation sums it all up:

Watch your thoughts, for they become your words.
Watch your words, for they become your actions.
Watch your actions, for they become your habits.
Watch your habits, for they become your character.
Watch your character, for it becomes your destiny.[4]

Scripture provides ample evidence of a man or woman's character becoming their destiny. In order to better understand the effect of habits, I investigated twenty-eight Biblical characters and charted my findings:

A Journey of Generations
Lessons on Change from God's Mighty Men and Women

God's Child	Scripture Passage	Change Point (+ or −)
Adam	Genesis 3:6	Ate the forbidden fruit (−)
Eve	Genesis 3:6	Ate the forbidden fruit (−)
Noah	Genesis 6:13–16	Built an ark (+)
Abram	Genesis 12:1–3	Left homeland for unknown places (+)
Abraham	Genesis 22	Willing to sacrifice his son (+)
Jacob	Genesis 32:22–32	Wrestles with an angel (+)
Moses	Exodus 3–4	Accepts the call to lead God's people (+)
Caleb	Numbers 13:30	Believes God (+)
Ten Spies	Numbers 13:26–33	Fears the giants in the land (−)
Moses	Numbers 20:1–13	Did things his own way (−)
Balaam	Numbers 22:21–24:25	Refuses to listen to God (−)
Achan	Joshua 7	Does not consult God (−)
Gideon	Judges 6	Demonstrates insecurity (+)
Samson	Judges 16	Succumbs to temptation (−)
Saul	1 Samuel 15:10–11	Disobeys God (−)
David	1 Samuel 17	Fights evil and trusts God (+)
Elijah	1 Kings 18:16–40	Demonstrates faith in God (+)
Job	Job	Prevails through suffering (+)
Daniel	Daniel 6	Persists in prayer (+)
Mary	Luke 1:26–38	Accepts God's will (+)
Simon Peter and Andrew	Matthew 4:18–22	Follows hard after God (+)
Woman with issue of blood	Mark 5:24–34	Perseveres through pain (+)
Jesus	Mark 14:35–36	Sacrifices his life (+)
Nicodemus	John 3:1–21	Receives new life in Christ (+)
Judas	Matthew 26:14–16	Pursues monetary gain (−)
Samaritan woman	John 4:1–26	Receives the Living Water (+)
Disciples	Acts 2	Filled with the Holy Spirit (+)
Saul (Paul)	Acts 9:1–19	Receives spiritual sight (+)

True change is a painstaking process. You can see that some of these men and women handled the change in a positive way, some in a negative way. (In the "Time in the Tower" section, you'll look further at these Bible personalities and see how their lessons can be applied to our lives.) All were required to be flexible—pliable in the hands of God.

Flexibility, that quality of being able to bend or yield to arguments, persuasions, or circumstances is a rare jewel in the crown of a rock-solid family. No two days will be alike. No two years will be alike. No two children will be alike. Rarely, if ever, does anything in a household stay the same. Life is constantly changing—I lovingly refer to this as "the ebb and flow of daily living." Bruce Barton, a congressman from New York in the late 1930s, gave us a clearer understanding of how important it is "to go with the flow," or to be flexible family members: "When you are through changing, you are through."[5]

At the onset of my parenting years, this was a difficult concept for me to grasp. It seemed just as I was getting into a routine with my children, they would change! Why do children do that? (Dumb question isn't it?) Every age brings a new set of dynamics and because of that I need to be flexible and ready to learn.

Being flexible is an area that needs our constant attention. Webster says *flexible* as "capable of being turned or forced from a straight line or form without breaking."[6] Think of a straight line, constantly moving forward into infinity. Very often, we are like that straight line. We have a plan and nothing is going to interfere with that plan. I thought I would be a dance teacher and own my own dance studio until I was well into my senior years. No one could have prepared me for the dramatic life change that forced me to sell my studio and stop dancing.

Life has a way of turning things upside down. What do we do when:

- Our husband loses his job and finances become strained?
- A disability emerges in our child?
- Someone close to us dies unexpectedly?
- A sudden illness forces Mom to months of bed rest?
- War is declared and duty calls a loved one to the other side of the world?
- _____ (you fill in the blank)

What do we do when the rapids of change force their way upon our families? I suggest six things:

1. Fall on your knees. Pray, *Lord, help us*. It is on our knees that we exchange our perspective for God's perspective. This divine exchange is the key to forward movement.
2. Slow down the pace of life. Take a step back in order to see the big picture. Give yourself permission to take a break and catch your breath.
3. Lock the door on life. Let your family draw close to one another, for a season. You may be misunderstood, but God understands. Well-intentioned friends and family often make the situation worse.
4. Silence the whirlwind. Change is a tornado at times—coming out of nowhere, spinning out of control.
5. Get your bearings. To "learn exactly where you are and in which direction you should proceed"[7] is the exact course of action necessary in such times.
6. Be flexible and make room for the adjustments that must follow.

For twelve years, my family lived in the dream house my husband built. In this home, nestled on two acres in the country, we raised our three children. Almost every day of those twelve years, I backed out of our driveway on Cedar Creek Lane and turned right at the stop sign to find my way into the

"This is an ingredient in God's plan of dealing with us. We are to enter a secret chamber of isolation in prayer and faith that is very fruitful. At certain times and in certain places, God will build a mysterious wall around us. He will take away all the supporters we customarily lean upon, and will remove our ordinary way of doing things. God will close us off to something divine, completely new and unexpected, and that cannot be understood by examining our previous circumstances. We will all be in a place where we do not know what is happening, where God is cutting the cloth of our lives by a new pattern, and thus where He causes us to look at Him."[8]

city. But on March 19, 2005, our convenient way to travel, known as the King's Highway Bridge, closed indefinitely. Concrete barricades and a huge Road Closed sign forced us to begin turning left every day—adding twenty to forty minutes to our daily commute. Now, even a quick trip to the grocery store was a big deal.

The first question on everyone's lips was, "What in the world are we going to do? Are they going to reopen the bridge?"

But the citizenry had absolutely no idea. The Virginia Department of Transportation and city officials couldn't seem to agree on a course of action. So, at that point, "our" bridge was closed indefinitely.

My husband and I prayed. We waited. We pondered the situation.

Sensing the Lord leading us to make a big move, we began to look at houses for sale in the area. On May 21, we put our house on the market. Two months later, a contract was negotiated and signed with our potential buyer. We then bought a new home, located in a more strategic place geographically, that would better suit the needs of our family's next season of life.

Unbeknownst to us, there were complications with the contract on our existing house and it fell through. Hence, our housing ordeal commenced. In a quandary as to why all this happened, we felt trapped in a whirlwind of opinions, suggestions, and questions. Amid the confusion, my husband, Rob, grew stronger and stronger, becoming the rock we all clung to. Convinced God would be faithful, and overwhelmed by the goodness of God to make provision for our family, Rob led us all to a new level of faith. Finding ourselves in unfamiliar territory was daunting, but oddly, it drew our family closer to God and to one another.

In order to bring about true and lasting change, one must have ample time to sit down and think—time without distractions. Sometimes life gets so noisy we forget how to listen. In studying this issue, I came across a beautiful passage in Isaiah 50:4–5: "The Sovereign LORD has given me an instructed tongue, to know the word that sustains the weary. He wakens me morning by morning, wakens my ear to listen like one being taught. The Sovereign LORD has opened my ears, and I have not been rebellious."

Life will force changes upon you and your family. This is a given. The metaphorical Road Closed sign shone as a message

---

"Light is given to us to know what next step we should take—just light enough and no more; a rim of light, hemmed in by darkness falling as a faint circle on our path. Shall we take the next step? We hesitate, because we cannot see the step beyond, and the next beyond; or because we fail to see the reason, and are not satisfied to act on the conviction of known duty. But so long as we refuse to act, that light cannot increase, but begins inevitably to decline. Obedience is the condition for its increase, nay, for its maintenance at all."[9]

from heaven to our family—it's time to make a change! Every time I looked at it, I couldn't help but smile. Day after day, I walked my usual two miles, stopping each day to pray. With my head resting on the big metal road sign, I conversed with God. "God, did you have to go to such extremes to get our attention? I mean, close our bridge? Why now, after seventy-seven years of operation? To force us to move in a new direction?"

I didn't hear an audible voice. I didn't hear angels blaring trumpets or shouting messages. But, I sensed the still, small voice of my heavenly Father. I sensed a deep peace. A peace that passes all understanding (see Philippians 4:7).

I believe that God orchestrated our circumstances—even the closing of our bridge. We thought we would live in our beautiful, quiet neighborhood forever. The closing of our bridge rocked our world and brought us to our knees. God wanted to move our family in a new direction. He wanted to stretch our faith and develop our spiritual muscles.

Pastor and author A.W. Tozer (1897–1963) wrote, "The widest thing in the universe is not space; it is the potential capacity of the human heart. Being made in the image of God, it is capable of almost unlimited extension in all directions. And one of the world's greatest tragedies is that we allow our hearts to shrink until there is room in them for little beside themselves."[10]

God's desire is to widen the capacity of the human heart to contain more of his spirit, in order that we will have a wider sphere of influence in this world. The enlargement process works from the inside out. It is very often accompanied by a purging—a spiritual stretching—a tear-laden process that cannot be avoided if we want to move forward in the ways of God. Take a moment and review the "Family Heart Checkup" chart in the Appendix.

As you review it, keep in mind the word *oppressive*. What word do you see tucked inside of *oppressive*? Yes, *press*. Derived from the Latin roots *ob* and *premo*, *oppress* means "to load or burden with unreasonable impositions; to overpower; to treat with unjust severity, rigor or hardship."[11] All these occupants—ego, pride, insecurity, inferiority, abuse, addiction, bitterness, materialism, anger, jealousy, criticism, fear, comparison, drivenness, selfishness—are inward, "me"-focused impositions that slow our growth and bring heaviness of heart. In order to effectively lead our families, we must seek God's help in evicting these occupants from our hearts.

Which of the behaviors listed above jumped out at you immediately? Investigate them further. Let's begin by choosing anger. Ask yourself:

- How do I react when a situation makes me angry?
- Do I slam doors? Cry? Yell? Withdraw into "the silent treatment" mode? Hit something? Open the refrigerator? Numb myself through shopping or other addictive behaviors?
- How can I manage this behavior and overcome its dominion in my life?
- Do I need professional help? An accountability partner?
- Am I being honest with myself? My spouse? Remember, we are being very honest with ourselves here. No more secrets. No more lies. No more masks.

As we evict these negative character qualities, we then must "put on the new" as described in Colossians 3:12: "Therefore, as God's chosen people, holy and dearly loved, clothe yourselves with compassion, kindness, humility, gentleness and patience." How different our homes would be if we really operated in all these virtues?

I am sure of one thing: this examination process isn't easy. *Trust me.* I've been there and will be there again.

Don't expect all the changes to come at once. Cast your ideals, preconceived notions of parenting, expectations of your children and your mate, and personal perfectionism at the feet of the One who will enable you to accomplish all that is required of you. Stress management experts Dr. Lew Childre and Bruce Cryer sum it all up for us: "Flexibility and adaptability do not happen just by reacting fast to new information. They arise from mental and emotional balance, the lack of attachment to specific outcomes, and putting care for self and others as a prime operating principle. Flexible attitudes build flexible physiology. Flexible physiology means more resilience in times of challenge or strain. Staying open—emotionally—ensures internal flexibility."[12] Balancing the scales of flexibility and order won't always be easy, but it is in their delicate balance that our fortresses of faith will be built, and built to last the test of time.

Time in the Tower

Think Change!

Take another look at **A Journey of Generations** chart (page 29). There are twenty-eight men and women whom God changed. Some handled the change in a positive manner, hence the "change point (+)," but some handled the change in a negative manner, hence the "change point (−)." Write down an area in your life that needs the power of the Holy Spirit to bring about change. Choose one man or woman from the list with whom you identify to study over the next few days or weeks. Read through that person's account and extract the principles that might help you. Write them down and study them, determining how to apply them in your life. Ask yourself:

- How did that person change?
- What effected the change?
- Can I learn anything from his or her experience?
- Is God requiring a similar change from me? What steps can I take to bring about the necessary change(s) in my life?

Notes

1. WorldofQuotes.com. http://www.worldofquotes.com/topic/habits/index.html (accessed February 26, 2007).

2. Rob Lebow, "Heart Quotes: Quotes of the Heart," *Heart Quotes Center.* http://www.heartquotes.net/Flexibility.html (accessed March 26, 2007).

3. Joan Lunden, *A Bend in the Road Is Not the End of the Road* (New York: William Morrow, 1998).

4. ThinkExist.com. http://thinkexist.com/search/searchquotation.asp?search=Watch+your+thoughts%3B+they+become+your+words.&q= (accessed May 18, 2007).

5. ThinkExist.com. http://thinkexist.com/quotation/when_you_are_through_changing-you_are_through/200125.html (accessed May 18, 2007).

6. Noah Webster, *An American Dictionary of the English Language* (New York: S. Converse, 1828). Facsimile first edition (Chesapeake, VA: Foundation for American Christian Education, 1967 and all subsequent editions).

7. *The American Heritage Dictionary of Idioms*, Houghton Mifflin Company, 1992. http://www.answers.com/topics/get-one-s-bearings, (accessed June 13, 2007).

8. Mrs. Charles Cowman, *Streams in the Desert* (Grand Rapids, MI: Zondervan, 1997), 143.

9. F. B. Meyer, *Moses* (Fort Washington, PA: Christian Literature Crusade, 1994), 42.

10. A. W. Tozer, *The Pursuit of God: The Human Thirst for the Divine* (Camp Hill, PA: Christian Publications Inc., 1993).

11. Noah Webster, *An American Dictionary of the English Language.*

12. Heart Quotes Center. http://www.heartquotes.net/Flexibility.html (accessed June 12, 2007).

3

ORDER
Stop the Madness!

> "Life in Modern-day America is essentially void of time and space. Not the Star Trek kind. The sanity kind. The time and space that once existed in the lives of people, who regularly lingered after dinner, helped the kids with homework, visited with the neighbors, sat on the lawn swing, went for long walks, dug in the garden, and always had a full night's sleep. People are exhausted. People are stressed. People are breaking the speed limit of life. People are overloaded. We need more time. We need more space. We need more reserves. We need more buffer. We need time to rest, and space to heal."[1]

People are breaking the speed limit of life." Does this statement ring true? Do you feel as though you are breaking the speed limit of life? Or perhaps the speed limit of life is breaking you? Why is it mothers and fathers need more time? Aren't there enough hours in the day?

Several years ago, I sat in my doctor's office and heard a prognosis that completely altered my life's passion and profession as a dance educator and drew me into a personal quest for deeper communion with God. For years I had suffered with back pain and severe headaches but thought this type of pain was normal for a dancer. But one

> Order must begin in the soul.

morning, my pain threshold broke and I couldn't get out of bed.

"Janell, you are going to the doctor," ordered my husband. So I did. I was told I had a back condition known as spondy-lolysthesis, a stress fracture within the middle part of my L5-S1 vertebrae. Stunned, I sat motionless, waiting for more direction.

"It's possible it's a congenital condition known as pars defect," the doctor said. "Janell, you are going to have to limit your dancing, maybe stop it all together. Whatever the case, you are definitely going to have to move through life in a much different way."

I stared, appalled. Dance was what I did. It was my joy, my passion, my life. Me, not dance? *Who am I without dance?* I thought.

"You definitely can't do that arching of the back anymore!" she commented.

"But I'm a dancer!" I exclaimed.

"You *were* a dancer. Now, you're a woman with serious back problems."

I cried all the way home. I recognized the pain in my chest as my heart shattering into little pieces.

When I got home, I went straight to my prayer closet. "Why, God? What are you doing to me? What do I do if I don't dance? What about all my students? What will they do? Where will they go to learn to dance for you? Fix it, God. Make my back whole. I know you can."

With a million questions streaming from my mouth, I finally wore myself out and lay facedown. It was here that I began my journey toward ordering my life. To an overachiever who thrives on doing things and doing them exceptionally well, the idea of resting or abiding (internally or externally) seemed completely outrageous and foreign.

Up to this point, I had considered resting as something for wimps or underachievers with no drive or motivation. It sounds so egotistical, I know, but I am being completely honest with you. When God began dealing with me, he revealed my selfishness and ego-driven motivations. Much of what I did "in his name" was actually self-serving and self-gratifying. The pats on the back and public affirmation fueled my dysfunction even more.

The French have an expression, *Recular pour mieux sauter,* meaning that you have to step back, retreat a little, if you're going to successfully jump over something. Want to jump across a ditch? You don't just walk to the edge and then leap. You walk to the edge, gauge the distance, and then retreat a bit to give yourself a full running start before you leap. You can't take the next step forward unless you take the time to step back first. Where will you get the strength to *sauter* (leap forward) if you can't allow yourself to *recular* (pull back)?[2]

We're going to step back now. We're going to rewind, suspend time, and take a good, long look at the condition of our lives and the lives of those with whom we live—physically, spiritually, emotionally, and naturally (i.e., our homes, our physical environment). In order to move forward, we must do this.

One of the greatest areas of conflict in many lives is found in this area: *order.* There isn't a great deal written on this topic, but it is at the very core of all of life's processes. We all know God is a God of order. He established the heavens and the earth according to an orderly system. His creativity was displayed through a systematic order of events. Reading through Genesis, we see this order in action: "on the first day," "on the second day," and so on.

God had a plan. He followed that plan. He completed his work. He rested. Twenty-four hours in a day—that is God's design. His ordered amount of time for us to accomplish our day's work. I tell my children all the time that God gives us twenty-four hours in which to accomplish all the day entails. I encourage them to listen as others comment, "There isn't enough time in the day." My response? "Oh, yes! God, our infinite source of wisdom, designed the day and that must be good enough for us." If we can't accomplish our agenda for the day, then we must step back, look it over, and make adjustments.

The overloaded, discontented lifestyle dictated by postmodern culture had seeped slowly and subtly into every facet of our lives—luring us away from authenticity and intimacy that God created us to have, both individually and corporately. We were not created "to do" but "to be" one with Christ, daily communing and relating to the One who created us in the first place. It isn't only a matter of simplification of lifestyle but sanctification of heart, mind, body, and soul. "Sanctification," writes theology professor Wayne Grudem, "is a progressive work of God and man that makes us more and more free from sin and like Christ in our actual lives."[3]

This truth confirms the reality I have witnessed in my own life and in the lives of countless men and women with whom I come in contact. One common theme seems to weave itself through every plea: Each one hungers after something deeper in life; all desire to push away the hustle and bustle in order to embrace the peace and power that a God-focused life provides. All hunger for a sense of order, but are lost in the chaos of our culture. This is where we step back. This is where we must "Think change!" This is where we make a plan, stop the madness, and pray.

You see, I personally believe with all my heart that God desires that we live a well-ordered, peace-filled, abundant life. It is his heart. How can I be so sure? By examining the Scriptures and studying the life of Jesus, whose life completely convinces me God doesn't want us frazzled, frustrated, and falling apart. Correct me if I am wrong, but I can't find one account in Scripture where Jesus exhibited any of those characteristics. He emulated a life of order. First Corinthians 14:33 describes it well: "God is not a God of disorder but of peace." Even when all hell broke loose in the Garden of Gethsemane (see Matthew 26:36–50), Jesus overcame his darkest hour and found strength in the presence of his Father. And it was this strength that calmed his severest storm, enabling him to press onward to fulfill his destiny.

Jesus had gone with his disciples to Gethsemane and said to them, "Sit here while I go over there and pray." He took Peter, James, and John with him, and he began to be sorrowful and troubled. Then he said to them, "My soul is overwhelmed with sorrow to the point of death. Stay here and keep watch with me."

Going a little farther, he fell with his face to the ground and prayed, "My Father, if it is possible, may this cup be taken from me. Yet not as I will, but as you will."

Then he returned to the three disciples and found them sleeping. "Could you men not keep watch with me for one hour?" he asked Peter. "Watch and pray so that you will not fall into temptation. The spirit is willing, but the body is weak."

He went away a second time and prayed, "My Father, if it is not possible for this cup to be taken away unless I drink it, may your will be done."

When he came back, he again found them sleeping, because their eyes were heavy. So he left them and went away once more and prayed the third time, saying the same thing.

Then he returned to the disciples and said to them, "Are you still sleeping and resting? Look, the hour is near, and the Son of Man is betrayed into the hands of sinners. Rise, let us go! Here comes my betrayer!"

God's desire is that we follow the example of his Son. Even in our darkest hours, our lowest moments, and our severest storms, we can find order in the chaos and peace amid the storm. "God's peace," writes theology professor Wayne Grudem, "means that in God's being and in his actions he is separate from all confusion and disorder, yet he is continually active in innumerable well-ordered, fully controlled, simultaneous actions." He continues, "This definition indicates that God's peace does not have to do with inactivity, but with ordered and controlled activity. To engage in infinite activity of this sort, of course, requires God's infinite wisdom, knowledge, and power. When we understand God's peace in this way we can see an imitation of this attribute of God not only in 'peace' as part of the fruit of the Spirit in Galatians 5:22–23, but also in the last-mentioned element in the fruit of the Spirit, namely, 'self-control.' "[4]

> Even in our darkest hours, our lowest moments, and our severest storms, we can find order in the chaos and peace amid the storm.

By now, you're asking, "How? How is this possible? How can I live an ordered life amid all the demands surrounding me? Sounds really good on paper but in reality, this is impossible." Well, let's take a step back. Let's increase our understanding of order and develop a plan for implementing the changes necessary to grow in this area.

What Is Order?

Order is "the regular disposition or methodical arrangement of things."[5] All creation demonstrates order. I think of the brown pelicans I watched one summer while vacationing in Hatteras, North Carolina. They flew in such a beautiful pattern of order . . . one leading . . . oth-

> When I see a flock of birds flying in their mesmerizing formation, I am reminded of the power of God's principle of order.

ers following. The lead pelican would flap once and soar . . . then the next . . . and the next . . . in the choreographed pattern danced by this flock of birds. They weren't fighting each other, trying to outdo one another, stressing out about who leads the pack or who wins the race, just working in a God-ordained fashion of flight. To this day, when I see a flock of birds flying in their mesmerizing formation, I am reminded of the power of God's principle of order.

Order must begin within the soul. God always, I believe, works from the inside to the outside. Anne Morrow Lindbergh, in her brilliant work, *The Gift of the Sea*, suggests, "This is the end toward which we could strive—to be the still axis within the revolving wheel of relationships, obligations and activities."[6] I fondly call this "the whirling wheel of activity." Do you feel as though your whirling wheel of activity is spinning madly? It can happen so quickly. Every "yes" is a spoke on the wheel. Before you know it, your wheel is overloaded with activities; they are all good, but are they all necessary? How can we bring order to the confusion, quietness to the chaos?

> Consistency is the warm blanket that wraps every day and fosters nurture, routine, and a sense of order.

Think for a moment upon the nucleus of Anne Morrow Lindbergh's statement: "the still axis within." A family will, at times, feel as though it is spinning out of control. Life gets busy. Very busy. But when we have ordered our world, we can remain calm and centered. May I suggest 1 Thessalonians 4:11–12 as a guideline for facilitating a greater sense of order within the realm of your soul? "Make it your ambition to lead a quiet life, to mind your own business and to work with your hands, just as we told you, so that your daily life may win the respect of outsiders and so that you will not be dependent on anybody."

Three things are noted within this Scripture passage that are highly significant when it comes to leading a well-ordered life.

1. Make it your ambition to lead a quiet life.

I am speaking from great experience here, for it has never been my ambition to lead a quiet life. Anyone who knows me would concur that I am anything but quiet. My friend Kathy and I were founding members of G.O.A.T.S.—Godly Overachievers Addicted to Stress. We were on the fast track—involved in a million things—until we ran out of steam! Kathy moved to Iowa—and left me behind. But, she keeps in contact with me, making sure I was sticking to our agreement to lead quieter lives.

So, for the last few years, God has been directing my path to this very place, demanding, as a good Father would, that I take full account of my activities, obligations, and responsibilities. He has required my full attention. After several years of tremendous physical challenge, I finally got the message: Slow down or burn out. Daily fatigue, as aforementioned, completely drained the energy and joy from my life, serving as a noose that slowly constricted my ability to cope and function. I had no choice. In order to take full account, I had to block off a portion of time to think over and outline the schedule of our family's activities. Use the simple chart in the "Time in the Tower" section at the end of this chapter.

2. Mind your own business.

My husband always cautions me to not "poke my nose" where it doesn't belong. In other words, "Don't get caught up in the drama, Janell. Hold your tongue and walk away," he wisely counsels. "If someone wants your opinion or needs your help, they will ask for it."

I am learning to wait until asked before offering my opinion. Good rule of thumb. For someone in the business of talking to others, this task was a difficult one. But, after following my husband's advice, truckloads of emotional clutter were deleted from my life, leaving me ample energy to complete my daily routine with renewed vigor. Does this mean I don't help others? Absolutely not. It does mean that I don't get involved in everybody's business. Sometimes it takes an iron will to turn away from a conversation or situation, but I know I must. "Walk away," I say to myself. "Save your energy. This is none of your business."

There is a huge difference between unsolicited involvement and making a solid contribution in someone's life. The beauty lies in knowing the difference:

Unsolicited Involvement	Solid Contribution
Unsolicited involvement leaves a spiritual mess.	A solid contribution leaves a spiritual legacy.
Unsolicited means "not asked for."[7]	*Contribution* means "giving."[8]
Synonyms: Unwelcome. Uncalled for.	Synonyms: Input. Involvement.
Consider the annoyance of an unsolicited telemarketing phone call during dinner. And the No Solicitation signs on businesses? They are there for a reason. Unwelcome visitors drain and distract.	Consider the beauty of friends who volunteer to plan, prepare, and serve a meal to guests in your home after a loved one's funeral. Their welcome arms offer a solid contribution. They ask for nothing in return.

Unsolicited involvement in the affairs of others tends to produce a quantity of relationships, but a lack of quality in those relationships. So, it is a question of breadth or depth. And intimate relationships require energy, devotion, and time. As human beings, we have a limited amount of energy. An inappropriate expenditure of this energy will result in emotional imbalance.

For years, I suffered with this malady, until I came to the realization that my relationships were completely out of order. I tried to be everybody's friend and ended up utterly exhausted. With the help of God, I chiseled away at the core of my problem and evaluated my quandary:

- How much time do I spend on the phone every day? Am I making good use of my time?
- Is it truly necessary conversation? Or is it idle gossip? Chitchat?
- Are all the places I am committed really where God wants me to devote my time and energy? Am I spread so thin that my attention is divided? My focus fractured?
- Am I poking my nose where it doesn't belong?
- Do I crave being involved in everything?
- Do I derive self-esteem from being needed by everyone? Being in the center of the drama? Being in the know?
- Does my family suffer from neglect because of the activities above?

I ask this because mine did. One day, while I was at work, my husband stopped by. The tears in his eyes said it all. "I miss you," he said. "I married you because I liked spending time with you. Something has to change." Here are some of the changes we agreed to:

- Discuss commitments, as a family, prior to saying "yes" or "no."
- Screen incoming calls. Establish a set amount of time for returning calls.
- Do not return every phone call, unless it begs returning. The world will rotate without your constant attention.

- Stay true to your highest calling as a spouse and parent.
- Be flexible when a real need arises.
- Focus on the task at hand. (We talked in great detail about the *fire of focus* in chapter one.)
- Apply what you have learned.

It's amazing what happens when we begin to mind our own business. A reservoir of energy surfaces—energy for the work God has called us to do. Late one summer, I agreed to assist with my daughter's varsity cheerleading squad. The head coach wanted me to choreograph a pom-pom routine for Homecoming.

"Sure, I can do that," I agreed, with no idea that my first book, the one you are holding, would be accepted for publishing.

In the midst of this exciting time, the head coach stepped down from her responsibilities, leaving the squad without a coach—right in the middle of Homecoming festivities and one month before a big competition.

Care to guess who was waiting in the wings? Me!

"Mom, you can't do this," cautioned my oldest daughter. "You have a full plate. What are you thinking?"

"I know. It doesn't make any sense. Normally I would say no, but I feel God leading me to stand in the gap. It won't be easy, but his ways aren't always easy. He will help me."

Two days later, I was the head coach of fourteen high school cheerleaders. I didn't ask for this position but clearly saw the opportunity. In the midst of cheers, chants, and metallic pom-

> A fortified home is a focused home.

poms, I was able to make a solid contribution in the lives of young women.

3. Don't compete with others.

Striving to get ahead can be positive, but very often we strive to excel for the wrong reasons. It brings unrest when accompanied by a need to prove ourselves, compete with others, or fill something within ourselves that only Jesus Christ can fill. I check myself by asking a few simple questions:

- What is the motivation for what I am doing?
- Are my motives love-based or performance-based?
- If no one in the whole world noticed what I did today, would God's praise be enough?

Okay, ouch! I know, these are not easy questions, but remember, honesty is mandatory when it comes to implementing real change. Yes, God sends encouragers to affirm our work at home—thank goodness—but our service must first be grounded in humility and love. Very often, we want to "do what everyone else is doing," or "what is expected of us," so we forego our sense of reason and good judgment, bringing stress and strain upon our homes.

A fortified home is a focused home. In *Shelter for the Spirit*, certified life coach Victoria Moran stresses that home must receive priority status:

> "A home is a signature, distinct and recognizable. The love put into it may be the greatest accomplishment of a lifetime."[9]

We live in a place and time when it takes courage and determination to give home priority status, or even realize that it might be a good idea to do so. Most of us are gone a lot, and when we do come home, we're often tired—weary from a variety of activities and torn by conflicting commitments. Sometimes we actually seek these activities out because they don't ask as much of us as the demands of home. Besides, achievement in the outer world is often accompanied by a level of fanfare that domestic accomplishments seldom receive. Even so, there are pioneers among us who are engaged in a sort of homesteading of the heart. These are young people who are redefining home for themselves after experiencing a familial environment that was frightening or belittling. These pioneers include all the people who are making day-to-day, domestic choices based on loving convictions. A home is a signature, distinct and recognizable. The love put into it may be the greatest accomplishment of a lifetime."[10]

Even though I'm aware that the love put into the home may be the greatest accomplishment of a lifetime, I have struggled year after year with a haunting feeling of failure. *Is this all my life is going to be? Grocery shopping? Cooking? Laundry? Chauffeuring my children? Waiting hours upon hours at lessons and practices?* Have you had those thoughts? But all that changed for me when I realized I am not only raising my children to be great human beings, but also am, in essence, affecting *their* children, and *their* children. My husband and I are building a legacy, a heritage, a future.

As you read through these words, may you sift through them, taking whatever pearls you might find that will enable you to strengthen your family. I believe with all my heart that the key to a strong family, and to life itself, is discipline, and order precedes discipline. We all make mistakes, we all "fall short of the glory of God" (Romans 3:23), but with God's sovereign grace flowing freely, we can become exactly who he has designed us to be.

Time in the Tower

Stop the Madness!

Read Genesis 1–3. Find five ways God demonstrates the principle of order. How do these acts show the importance of order? Now, find five ways you can bring order into your home—spiritual, emotional, and/or physical. Be very practical.

For example, you might say, "Our schedules are way too

hectic. We need to sit down and evaluate the level of activities, responsibilities, and obligations of each family member—from the youngest to the oldest."

Fill in the chart below. After you are done, begin the difficult process of making changes. Remember Foundation Stone 2, *Think Change*! You can do this—I know you can!

Family Member (List each family member and his/her activities, responsibilities, and obligations.)	Activities, Responsibilities, and Obligations	Assessment (Remember, there are many seasons in life—can this activity, responsibility, or obligation wait until another season—perhaps a better season for the family as a whole?)

Notes

1. Richard Swenson, *The Overload Syndrome* (Colorado Springs: NavPress, 1999), 11.

2. Mira Kirshenbaum, *The Gift of a Year* (New York: Plume Books, 2001).

3. Wayne Grudem, *Systematic Theology* (Leicester, UK, and Grand

Rapids, MI: InterVarsity and Zondervan, 1994), 746.

4. Ibid., 203.

5. Noah Webster, *An American Dictionary of the English Language* (New York: S. Converse, 1828). Facsimile first edition (Chesapeake, VA: Foundation for American Christian Education, 1967 and all subsequent editions).

6. Anne M. Lindbergh, *The Gift of the Sea* (New York: Pantheon, 1991), 45.

7. Noah Webster, *An American Dictionary of the English Language.*

8. Ibid.

9. Victoria Moran, *Shelter for the Spirit* (New York: Harper Perennial, 1997), 10–11.

10. Ibid.

ORGANIZATION
Take Baby Steps!

> "When faced with a mountain, I WILL NOT QUIT!
> I will keep on striving until I climb over, find a pass through,
>   tunnel underneath,
> or simply stay and turn that mountain into a gold mine with
>   God's help."[1]

Repeat after me: "SLAY THE GIANT!" Write these words on a 4 × 6 index card and place it on your refrigerator door. Addressing the subject of organization is like taking on Goliath, because we Americans have so many things. Christine Field offers this sage advice:

> Don't confuse orderliness with rigidity or inflexibility. Having a plan isn't a prison; it's a lifesaver. Organization and routine also help our children feel secure. When our surroundings are reasonably orderly and our children know what to expect from the day, they feel safe and grounded—and more able to focus on the task at hand—whatever that might be.[2]

Are you ready to assess the organizational status of your home? Ask yourself the following questions:

1. Is my home a "palace of peace," a "castle of chaos," or a "dungeon of drudgery"?
2. Am I the "queen of clean"? the "princess of packrats"? Or a "servant of slothfulness"?
3. What is my dream for my family? My life? My house? Do I long for seven sprawling acres? Or 750 square feet in Manhattan? Or what?
4. What space in my current living environment needs the most attention? (If you don't address this issue now, more than likely, once you enter your dream living environment, this problem will come with you.) Clutter is like a bad cold, it won't go away by itself.
5. Is there a habit I would like to break, or begin, in my daily routine? If I could get started thirty minutes earlier every day, I would have better control over my life. I need to hit the snooze button two fewer times!

Having twin babies, a four-year-old, and a 1,500-square-foot house propelled my search for gaining mastery over my living environment. Then I received another incentive to organize in the aftermath of my mother-in-law's sudden death. Having to sort through all her belongings, drawer by drawer, was daunting. I remember crying, asking myself, "If I died today, would I want my loved ones to see the messes I have shoved in my dresser, closets, etc.?"

Being organized is not about cleaning up messes or hiding clutter. It's about finding a system of organization that is right, one that will help transform a "castle of chaos" into a "palace of peace." But, before we go any further, please repeat after me: *Take baby steps!*

Julie Morgenstern offers us a great working definition of organization: "Organization is the process by which we create environments that enable us to live, work and relax exactly as we want to. When we are organized, our homes, offices, and schedules reflect and encourage who we are, what we want, and where we are going."[3]

The very definitions of the word *organize* support this: "To construct so that one part may cooperate with another. To distribute into suitable parts and appoint proper officers, so that the whole may act as one body."[4]

I don't know about you, but there are days when I feel as though I am at war with my home. Nothing seems to be cooperating. It doesn't take long for things to get disheveled. Years ago, in my angst and frustration, I took action.

First, I created a motto. This motto is the first weapon in my "Operation Organize" arsenal:

CLEAN IT UP!

Commit to a plan	**I**mplement intentional living	**U**se a fifteen-minute spruce-up
Lean on God's power	**T**rain family members	**P**ace yourself, Prune
Emerge energized		activities, and
Act immediately		Provide time
Never quit		

1. Commit to a plan.

Look at the answers to the questions I asked near the beginning of this chapter. Your answers will indicate the action you take. What is important to you? Start there. Take baby steps toward fulfilling the vision you have for your home and family. You are weaving your family mission statement and the vision for your home into a beautiful tapestry. Personal growth trainer Laurie Beth Jones writes, "Jesus did not live according to a written plan. But his vision did shape each day's activities—what he would do, what he would not do. Only in retrospect could it resemble a formal business plan."[5]

Twenty years ago, I didn't have a formal plan, either, but I had a vision. This vision shaped my dreams. Once again, this isn't anything cumbersome or complicated, but merely weighing options and devising concrete direction.

2. Lean on God's power.

I can't do anything without God's help. Oh, I try, but it never goes as well. David slew Goliath because of his immense trust in the power of the living God. "You come against me with sword and spear and javelin," David bellows, "but I come against you in the name of the LORD Almighty, the God of the armies of Israel, whom you have defied" (1 Samuel 17:45). We have already established that organizing our homes is like going up against Goliath, so obviously we need to attack our issue with the same fervor as David did his. Start the battle on your knees.

3. Emerge energized.

Prayer is spiritual oxygen. It will take energy, both physical and spiritual, to organize your home environment. The Holy Spirit will give you ample energy to carry out this task. "How can you be so sure?" you ask. Zechariah 4:6 tells me, " 'Not by might nor by power, but by my Spirit,' says the LORD Almighty." Herein lies my one-sentence directive for the task at hand: *God will give you the strength you need to organize your home.*

> "How does a project get to be a year behind schedule? One day at a time."[6]

4. Act immediately.

Time is of the essence. "How wonderful it is that nobody need wait a single moment," writes Anne Frank, "before starting to improve the world."[7] Little did Anne Frank know that she wouldn't have a lifetime of single moments. Her life abruptly ended as a result of Adolf Hitler's World War II concentration

"How true Daddy's words were when he said: all children must look after their own upbringing. Parents can only give good advice or put them on the right paths, but the final forming of a person's character lies in their own hands."[8]

camps. You have to seize the day and take control of your home environments—today. Improve your world by taking baby steps. Begin the process. Don't wait until you feel like it. Moods cannot serve as the barometer for beginning this task.

5. Never quit.

Churchill said it best: "Never, never, never quit." When you feel like quitting, remember these four principles:

Q = Quit whining.
U = Unite forces—call in help.
I = Imagine your dream living environment.
T = Take a short (and I emphasize *short*) break and treat yourself.

6. Implement intentional living.

Intentional means "deliberate, on purpose, calculated, premeditated."[9] The only way to conquer Goliath is by taking deliberate action. David went to the riverbed and chose five smooth stones. He walked toward the battle line. He challenged Goliath. He slew Goliath. All premeditated actions. Here are a few ideas about implementing intentional living:

- Create a budget for organization. Forego fancy coffees, fast food meals, DVD rentals, etc., in order to save money for the organization of your home. This is an investment in your future.
- Complete "Operation Organize" in six to twelve months. Rally the troops.

- Don't talk about the program. Do it.
- Clean out one drawer a day. One closet a month, etc.
- Stay away from any shopping experience that will tempt you to buy unnecessary decorations, trinkets, odds and ends, etc., for your home.
- Be accountable to one person. Join forces with a friend, relative, or organization specialist who will hold you accountable.

> Implement the Many Hands Principle. "Every family member must be committed and cooperative—from the youngest to the oldest!"[10]

7. Train family members.

This is one of the hardest parts of the process. Affectionately, I call this "The Many Hands Principle,"[11] because "large tasks become small when divided among several people."[12]

My friend, Ruth, knew the power in this principle. Frustrated and overwhelmed, she came by to share how it took her thirty minutes one afternoon to train Evelyn, her two-year-old, to put away her toys.

"She screamed and screamed," Ruth told me. "I really wanted to quit. But, I knew that she understood what I was saying. After thirty minutes, she quieted down, put the toys away, and hugged me."

"Wow, Ruth, I am really impressed," I applauded. "You're amazing. Keep up the great work. She will thank you one day. I promise."

Ruth understands that in order to make her home environment a sanctuary, her family must work as a team. Ephesians 4:16 records, "From him [Jesus] the whole body, joined and held together by every supporting ligament, grows and builds itself up in love, as each part does its work." Teamwork is most essential to the success of an organizing program. Every family member must be committed and cooperative, from the youngest to the oldest. Parent, this will be the most challenging aspect of implementation—training your children to work. Make it fun. Make it rewarding. For resources on this subject, check out www.resources.family.org. Do a search on "chores" and see what you find.

At the end of this chapter, I have provided "The Lesson of Little Things"—a simple, practical guide to begin training your children from a very young age to be organized. It can be done. When you are frustrated and frazzled, walk over to your refrigerator door, where you've posted your 4 × 6 organizational slogan, and read it aloud: "SLAY THE GIANT!"

8. Use a fifteen-minute spruce-up.

Every day, our family performs the "Fifteen-Minute Shake It Down and Sweep It Up!" Take fifteen minutes to sweep through the house:

- Clean one horizontal surface.
- Sort paper(s). File, throw away, or pin them to the Command Central bulletin board, etc. Follow the OHIO System—Only Handle It Once. When I retrieve the mail, I immediately look through it, tossing any unwanted pieces in the trash, and place the rest in the mail basket, which we keep in the kitchen. Then, once or twice a week, my husband goes through the mail basket and repeats the process.
- Return shoes, clothing, coats, etc., to closets, storage units, mud room.
- Wash dirty dishes. I run the dishwasher twice a day—in the morning and before I go to bed. Whoever has a minute empties it.

Upkeep is ongoing. If I don't feel like putting something away, I remind myself that sooner is better than later. A little internal pep talk works wonders.

9. Pace yourself, prune activities, and provide time.

The "3 Ps" are the second weapon in my organizational arsenal. Psalm 90:12 says, "Teach us to number our days aright, that we may gain a heart of wisdom." It takes time to bring order into our homes and time to keep it there. Find a day, a week, a season of time, where you can shut yourself off from the hurry of life to get organized, or at least to develop a plan of action. Wage an all-out assault on the war zone. Mark off a significant amount of time to get this initial work done. Perhaps you could hire a sitter or recruit family and friends to watch the children for a while, so you can work.

Are you ready to kill the giant? Once and for all? Okay, where do you start? At the beginning with the basics. You must repeat to yourself, *"Take baby steps!"* You can't and won't organize the entire house in a day. It will take time. Find one area that needs immediate attention and begin there. If you can afford to hire an organizational specialist, it might be money well spent. If you can't afford to hire an organizational specialist, here are some suggestions.

Improve the efficiency of your home. Key word: SIMPLIFY. Read some of the books suggested in the resource section and outline several different methods or approaches to simplification. Ask yourself:

1. Can I live without this item I am about to purchase?
2. Will it be in next year's garage sale?

> "Clutter is like a gnat circling around your head. You swat it, but unless you get it, it buzzes around and continues to annoy you. And just when you think you've got clutter under control, things start to pile up again. The gnat is back, once again, circling your head."[13]

3. Is there a place in my home for this object?
4. Why do I need this item? Will it make my life easier in any way?
5. Do I have a friend(s) with a gift for organization and administration?

If you can't do this alone, call in an objective person to assist you in the process. Victoria Moran suggests going through every room, with pencil and paper in hand, writing down all those items that feed your soul and nurture your spirit, eliminating everything else.

Recall your family mission. If you haven't already sat down with your spouse and created a family mission statement, this is the time to do it (see chapter one). Our mission statement is "TO STAND STRONG, TRUE, AND ABLE AS A FAMILY OF FAITH."

Identify the areas of your home and the items that are most essential to the well-being of every family member. Every family has a unique personality and mission. For example, home-schooling was a major part of our family dynamic, so I needed a homeschool room that was functional, stimulating, well-organized, and conducive to learning.

We have only scratched the surface of this enormous topic, but I hope you have gleaned at least one helpful idea. Purposing to point you in the right direction, I leave you with a simple, yet profound, truth in Proverbs 15:6: "The house of the righteous contains great treasure."

Great treasure. Isn't that beautiful? My home—your home—full of great treasure. Crown each room in your home with prayer, inviting joy, laughter, peace, grace, patience, faith, cooperation, vision, etc., to take up permanent residence. Remember that your home is a signature and may be the greatest achievement of your life.

The Lesson of Little Things

A young mother once asked me in frustration, "When do I begin training my little one to do these things? Do I just keep picking up her toys at the end of the day until she's old enough to do it herself? How much can I expect from her?"

After sharing with her the many schools of thought on this subject, I replied, "Now! Today is the day!" Begin dialoguing with your little one(s). You say, "Today, we are going to learn "The Lesson of Little Things.""

This training begins from *Day One* of their life here on earth! From the moment they are born, we begin training. Remember one thing in all of this—*more is caught than taught.* Children learn by example.

Around age two—or perhaps even earlier, depending on the child—assign a time every day to open God's Word and read from it. (My personal all-time favorite is *The Bible in Pictures for Little Eyes* by Kenneth N. Taylor, available on www.amazon.com. The older version is my personal choice due to its beautiful artwork. The newer version uses more cartoon-like illustrations.)

Day One: Read the Creation account found in Genesis 1–3 (and in *The Bible in Pictures for Little Eyes* on pages 7–10). Then tell your child something like this:

"God had a place for every creature . . . no matter how big or how small. He put the sun in the morning sky, the moon in the evening sky, the birds in the air, the fish in the sea, and the animals on land. They each had a specific place to be. Where is your place, little Susie, in God's big world?" She might respond, "Here." "Yes, right here in our home. God placed you here. So, we need to take care of your special place. It is very, very special. Let's start today. Let's make our room neat and tidy. This will please God."

Day Two: Read the account of Noah's Ark found in Genesis 6 and 7 (and in *The Bible in Pictures for Little Eyes* on pages 12–15). Tell your child:

"When God told Noah to build a boat, he also told him exactly how to build the boat. It took Noah a long, long time to build his boat. I am sure there were times when Noah wanted to quit, but he wanted to please God, so he kept on building! Susie, God wants us to keep our home and room clean. He wants us to pick up our toys and put them where they belong. We please God when we keep things neat and tidy. So, even when we're tired, we need to remember to put our things away. Then we can rest!"

Day Three: Read and discuss Matthew 25:14–29: "Well done, good and faithful servant! You have been faithful with a few things; I will put you in charge of many things." A big Scripture for a little soul? Yes, but little souls have a great capacity to learn and understand far more than we give them credit for. Oftentimes, I use *The Message* by Eugene Peterson to interpret these difficult passages. This modern version gives great insight and reads like a story.

First SHOW, then TELL. Choose one repetitive phrase that will be embedded into their heart, such as "Everything has a place; everything has a space" or "Remember the lesson of the little things!" or "God has a home for everything you own!" After laying the foundation of organization with them, all that is left to do is PRACTICE. Remain committed and constant in your efforts.

Time in the Tower

Take Baby Steps!

1. Is your house a Palace of Peace, a Castle of Chaos, or a Dungeon of Drudgery? (Remember, complete honesty is the beginning of true change. No one is going to judge your response except God and you, right?)

2. What one area in your home needs the most attention? What one baby step can you take today to begin your personal

home improvement? Be specific. My first baby step was the junk drawer next to my refrigerator. When I threw away the handfuls of refrigerator magnets collected over twelve years, I had an intense feeling of liberation. Once I knew how good it felt to have order, I kept going. Don't laugh! Order brings a great sense of relief. I always tell my children, "Little piles of laundry, little loads of dishes, little plots of weeds." Remember, *Take baby steps.*

3. What one baby step can you take to begin training your children to have an ordered living space? For example, go to the store and purchase storage bins. Label the bins: balls, building blocks, puzzles, etc. Begin training Susie or Bobby in "The Lesson of the Little Things."

Notes

1. Robert H. Schuller, "God Never Quits on You!" *New Hope*, www.newhopenow.com/schuller/thinking/sermom_2.html. (accessed June 14, 2007).

2. Christine M. Field, *Help for the Harried Homeschooler: A Practical Guide to Balancing Your Child's Education with the Rest of Your Life* (Colorado Springs: WaterBrook Press, 2002), 25.

3. Julie Morgenstern, *Organizing from the Inside Out: The Foolproof System of Organizing Your Home, Your Office, and Your Life* (New York: Owl Books, 2004), 3.

4. Noah Webster, *An American Dictionary of the English Language* (New York: S. Converse, 1828). Facsimile first edition (Chesapeake, VA: Foundation for American Christian Education, 1967 and all subsequent editions).

5. Laurie Beth Jones, *Jesus Entrepreneur* (New York: Three Rivers Press, 2002), 110.

6. Fred Brooks, Thinkexist.com, http://thinkexist.com/quotes/fred_brooks/.

7. Anne Frank, Brainyquotes.com, http://brainyquote.com/quotes/authors/a/anne_frank.html.

8. Ibid.

9. Encarta Dictionary, http://encarta.msn.com/dictionary_/intentional.html.

10. Bartleby.com, *The New Dictionary of Cultural Literacy.* http://www.bartleby.com/59/3/manyhandsmak.html (accessed March 29, 2007).

11. Ibid.

12. Ibid.

13. Christine M. Field, *Help for the Harried Homeschooler,* 25.

MARRIAGE
Today Is Fresh, but Tomorrow Will Be Fresher!

"Research confirms the importance of human bonds: without relationships we humans wither and die, both emotionally and physically. The quality of our life diminishes when there is no one to share it with—family, friends, or spouse. We were created for relationships. Everything about us was designed to live in close community and interaction with others. We certainly were not designed to go through life emotionally disconnected. And when we marry, an important and lifelong bond is formed—the connection between us and our spouse."[1]

Experts agree that the greatest gift a husband and wife can give their children is a happy marriage. Jay Kesler, former president of Youth for Christ, says:

> The primary relationship between a husband and a wife is the foundation on which kids build their sense of security, their identity, and learn to relate to others. This prepares them to eventually relate to their own spouse. Couples are

virtually helpless in relating to one another in later life if they have not observed a healthy relationship between their parents. In fact, it is only through a great deal of effort and relearning that people are able to overcome a dysfunctional family life. Therefore I repeat: the relationship between husband and wife is primary. Kids need to understand that mom and dad have something special going on. They need to know that your marriage is solid and that there is nothing anybody can do to divide you from one another.[2]

Jay Kesler's words ring true—it takes a great deal of effort and relearning in order to overcome a dysfunctional family of origin. Both my husband and I were raised in the home of alcoholic fathers. Having strong mothers, a strong faith, and a gracious, redeeming God has enabled us to face our difficulties and somehow surmount the residual effects of this type of home environment.

God initiated the marriage covenant. It was his idea. Genesis 2:7 records God's creation of man. It continues as God placed man, Adam, in the Garden of Eden to work it and take care of it. But something happened. God saw that it was not good for Adam to be alone. Genesis 2:18–25 records the creation of a helpmate for man. While Adam slept, God created a woman, Eve, for him. Now, Adam was complete. In the same way I complete my husband. Two halves become one whole.

So many times we forget this essential truth. Marriage is a partnership in every sense of the word. Two hearts join together to complete one another. It seems that the pace of the twenty-first century has eroded this vital principle. How many days do we pass our mates in the hallway or in the driveway with a quick glance or smile—so rushed we can't even pause for a hug? How many days are we so engrossed in our children, our projects, our planning, or outside activities that we don't even see each other?

This happened to me. After months of disconnection, my husband quietly said, "Where are you? I miss you. Do you think you could schedule me in?"

Stunned, it was almost as if I heard the Lord saying the same thing. "Where are you, Janell? I miss you. Do you think you could schedule me in?"

Pained by this confrontation, I remembered the words of God to his beloved creation, Adam, in Genesis 3:9: "Where are you?" God always communed with Adam in the cool of the evening. That's all my husband wanted—to commune with me in the cool of the evening. I was deeply moved by my husband's teary eyes and humble request. From that day forward, we penciled in time for one another.

One very special time was spent in St. Andrews, Scotland, celebrating our twenty-second wedding anniversary. Night after night, we stayed glued to the television to hear the weather man consistently repeat in his thick, Scottish accent, "Today was fresh, but tomorrow will be fresher!" I couldn't wait until 10:30 p.m. to hear it again. His gusto was infectious! The word *fresh* revolved in my mind. No matter where we traveled—castles, crags, or crowded streets—we would jokingly remind ourselves how "fresh" it felt outside—and how tomorrow would be "fresher!"

Your marriage should be full of life—"fresh today, fresher tomorrow." In the acrostic FRESH I offer five power-packed principles that will help keep your marriage fresh:

F = Financial freedom breeds a fresh atmosphere.
R = Remember, the little things are really the big things.
E = Experience life together—not two halves, but one whole.
S = Spend time developing your spiritual lives.
H = Halt harsh communication.

First and foremost, financial freedom breeds a fresh atmosphere in the home environment. Okay, I know this hurts.

Proverbs 31:10–12 (MSG) clarifies, "A good woman is hard to find, and worth far more than diamonds. Her husband trusts her without reserve, and never has a reason to regret it. Never spiteful, she treats him generously all her life long . . . She keeps an eye on everyone in her household, and keeps them all busy and productive." Don't we all want our spouse to trust us without reserve when it comes to spending money?

My husband regularly deposits his paycheck into our account and trusts that I will manage the money by paying the bills, purchasing groceries and household necessities, etc. He doesn't expect me to spend the day at the spa, charge new outfits for a dinner party, or take the children to Chuck E. Cheese every day . . . you get the picture. He expects that I spend money wisely.

The greatest lesson he has taught me over the years is that there will be times of surplus and times of deficit. Remember that contentment is the fruit of focus. Rethink Paul's exhortation in Philippians 4:11–13, in light of family finances: "I am not saying this because I am in need, for I have learned to be content whatever the circumstances. I know what it is to be in need, and I know what it is to have plenty. I have learned the secret of being content in any and every situation, whether well fed or hungry, whether living in plenty or in want. I can do everything through him who gives me strength."

> We have a need.
> Trusting God to meet our need + Resting in his promises = Contentment

This little, seven-letter word, *content,* is an enigma. In a world where everything is available at the click of a mouse, contentment seems almost a foreign concept. Because we can always get more, we are never content with what we have. If I want a new sweater, *click.* Earrings to match, *click.* The latest golf clubs, *click.* If I can't find something, Google will. All this without ever leaving my comfortable chair or opening my wallet—all I have to do is memorize my charge card number. Isn't it amazing how much trouble a little piece of plastic can cause?

Sinclair Ferguson writes,

> Christians today live in a society which is permeated by a spirit of discontentment . . . Greed has destroyed gratitude, getting has replaced giving. But in the pursuit of self-sufficiency we have lost our way. We have developed spirits driven forward to gain more, incapable of slowing, stopping and remembering that those who sow the wind reap the whirlwind. That ethos can easily influence. It is time to pause and ask, "Am I content, in Christ?" If not, it is the first thing I need to begin to relearn.[3]

(See "Developing an Attitude of Gratitude" in the Appendix.)

The Israelites had to learn and relearn the lesson of contentment. While wandering in the desert for forty years, they witnessed firsthand the power of God to provide for their every need. They were hungry? *Poof!* There was food (see Exodus 16). For forty years, to be exact, God provided the Israelites with food. Manna in the morning and quail in the evening. Enough for the day. No more. No less. They were thirsty? *Poof!* There was water (see Exodus 17).

Rob and I have had tough times, when we didn't know where in the world the money was coming from. But a dear former pastor wisely counseled us in our early years of marriage that it is still imperative to have at least one date a month and three short honeymoons a year.

How in the world is this possible? I remember thinking. *We have three small children and a very tight budget.*

Well, I am here to tell you it is possible. We spent our first anniversary at a campground with mosquitoes and geckos, where we slept in the back of my husband's van. We stayed in cheap—yes, *cheap*—hotels, packed meager lunches and picnicked at a local park, swapped babysitting hours with other couples and had quiet time at home, etc. Really, the options are endless and affordable. I know it takes creative energy, but in order to assure a lasting, fulfilling relationship we have to make the effort.

Mary, played by Donna Reed in Frank Capra's *It's a Wonderful Life*, knows all about making the effort to create special moments in a marriage. George Bailey (Jimmy Stewart), Mary's brand-new husband, lost all their honeymoon money trying to save his "ol' savings and loan" from being taken over by mean Mr. Potter. But Mary didn't let this ruin her honeymoon night. She was determined to not let a bad situation get the best of her. She transformed an old, rickety mansion into a tropical paradise! She even rigged up a rotisserie on which to cook their first dinner as man and wife. The result: one happy couple. One happy honeymoon night. It's that simple. There's a Mary Bailey inside each of us. See what you can do with a little thought and elbow grease!

So, Rob and I have had tough times. But, we have had great times, too. Which do I prefer? You guess. Five-star hotels don't have geckos in the shower. But somehow the tough times develop a deep-seated friendship. Having to trust God day by day is not easy, but it's essential to growth. This deep-seated trust in God breeds reliance and security. Even in the tough times, I don't have to eat manna and quail for forty years, but something tells me that those who rested in this provision were deeply content. Somehow they learned to do something special with that manna. Today, Martha Stewart would publish "100 Ways to Magnificent Manna Meals."

Safeguarding your spending habits will safeguard your marriages. Be wise. Be frugal. Be alert to all the subtle ways the money in your bank account slips away. Somehow, when there are no money burdens, a certain rest comes over the family. A deep sense of contentment hovers over the home, making it a haven from the chaos of overdrafts, the drain of debt, and an end-of-the-month financial fiasco.

I don't need all the things I think I need. I don't have dining room furniture. My husband promises that when the money is in the bank, we'll make our dining room both beautiful and welcoming. It has taught me to depend on my gracious neighbor, who has opened her beautiful home to my family on many occasions. We have broken bread in their home and eaten "together with glad and sincere hearts, praising God" (Acts 2:46–47). When the time is right, I will get a beautiful dining room suite—without three years of payments attached to it.

Second, remember the little things are really the big things. Ask, "How can I bless my mate? Focus on how you can be a blessing to your spouse rather than how your spouse should be a blessing to you. If both of you have the same giving attitude, you will both be blessed. But don't wait for your spouse to bless you. When you focus on getting your needs met through your spouse instead of from God, you will always come up short."[4] Love notes, phone calls, flowers, fifteen-minute time-outs from the children, dates, candlelight coffee breaks, secret rendezvous while the children are napping, sensual messages on the mirror in your private bathroom (until the children learn to read), etc. You get the idea. Don't forget—the small things are really the big things.

My husband is a master at *real* love. I suppose that is how he won my heart in the beginning. One Mother's Day, years ago, I awoke to find "Happy Mother's Day" mowed—yes, you read that right, MOWED—into the front yard of our house. From my second-story bedroom window, I could look down and see the message. I was stunned. *How in the world did he mow "Happy Mother's Day" into the lawn?* I couldn't fathom anyone doing something like that for me.

For weeks I had been on his case about mowing the lawn, so I felt terrible. *Why won't he cut the grass? It looks horrible!*

What will people think? Doesn't he care about me? Every time I nagged, he came up with some excuse. So, I stewed. And stewed. And stewed. Needless to say, Mother's Day morning I repented! All I could see was a messy yard. All my husband saw was a masterpiece in the making. I wish I had an aerial photo of this labor of love, but I don't. I only have a memory of how very much my husband cares about the little things in life.

Third, experience life as one whole—not two halves. Keep a storehouse of energy for intimacy and connection.

In the Garden of Eden (see Genesis 1 and 2), God had a plan. Upon creating the man, God realized Adam was lonely and needed some companionship. After all, Adam had named all of the animals—each of which had a mate. So, to solve the problem, he created man's companion, known to us as "woman." God took a rib out of the man and fashioned the woman from that rib. Now, man was complete. And God saw that this arrangement was not just good, but very good.

Let's face it, though—becoming one flesh is no picnic. When you decide to walk down the aisle and say your marriage vows, you make a decision—a strong commitment—to begin living a selfless life. Marriage requires a 100 percent giving of self at all times. It is hard, I know, but this truth will revolutionize your day-to-day living experience. Who likes to die to self? Who likes to place someone else's needs above their own? I know I die hard when it comes to being selfless.

But we must guard our inner resources. If we fall into bed drained, on a consistent basis, with nothing left to give, we are doing too much. Prune activities, obligations, and responsibilities. No matter how worthy, how great, how important, there is nothing more important than your marriage. Nothing.

Dr. John Gottman, pioneer of relationship research, interviewed more than seven hundred couples, recording their interactions and monitoring their heart rate and stress levels in his "Love Lab." His discovery was that "happy marriages are based on deep friendship."[5] And I add *intimacy*—spirit, soul, and body. Suddenly, two halves become one whole. If I am busy in one direction and my husband is busy in the opposite direction, when will our lives intersect? How can intimacy, on any level, happen? Intimacy is all about becoming one whole.

Intimacy, derived from the Latin root *intimus*, meaning "within," is defined as "inmost, inward, near, close in friendship."[6] My husband says to me all the time, "I married you because I enjoy being with you." Isn't that the essence of God's heart in Genesis, "communing in the cool of the day"? How can we give to one another if we are emotionally, physically, and spiritually drained? It is impossible. Times may come where normalcy is stalled or interrupted due to a death in the family, a busy time with work, a deployment, a new baby, caring for an elderly parent, etc., but this should be for a season, and special care and understanding given during this period.

After all these years, I have a built-in sensor that alerts me to the fact that my marital relationship needs attention. Agitation rears its ugly head, and I know it is time to lay aside the hurriedness and sit down next to my husband. Life sails more smoothly when my husband and I are nurturing our intimate relationship. It's funny—he hears me better, he listens to me better, and he supports me better. It's as simple as that.

Play together. Laugh. Stay young. Remember the time when you were falling in love? Take the time to be together. Quick glances across the room. A touch on the back when walking through a crowded mall. Opening the door for her. Tucking a love note in his lunch bag.

My husband and I rented a small garage house to a young pastor and his bride. I marveled at their ability to find small pockets of time to play together. Lying in the grass on a blanket reading a book to each other. Sipping coffee on their little deck. Playing badminton and croquet with friends—or alone! Weeding the garden and planting flowers. Seemingly little acts of recreation reap big rewards in the strengthening of the marital bond.

"Hug and kiss ten times a day," shouted motivational guru Zig Ziglar at a Valentine's Day event my husband and I attended. "That seems like such a silly prescription for marriage boredom," he added, "but I've been kissing my redhead for many, many years now. She doesn't seem to mind."

As I remember, it was the best money ever spent on a Valentine's Day date. Ziglar assured each of us that if we implemented this simple practice in our marriage courtship, we would both be happier and more fulfilled. Another study proved that men who were kissed prior to leaving for work were more productive and content. Sound silly? Try it! I challenge you!

Fourth, spend time developing your spiritual lives. Because we are spirit, soul, and body, we cannot neglect the spiritual aspect of our marriage. Gary Thomas challenges all married couples in his book *A Sacred Marriage*. "What if God designed marriage to make us holy more than to make us happy?"[7] he asks.

Whether this question touches you or not, I merely offer it as food for thought. I am sure of only one thing—without God in my marriage, I'd be lost. I will even go out on a limb and say that my marriage may not have succeeded without the assistance of the Almighty. I fell in love with Rob for many reasons—primarily for the Christian character he demonstrated. Rob was a man after God's heart. He was humble, kind, and faithful. He was unlike any man I had ever been involved with before. The spiritual disciplines of prayer and Bible study were evident.

It seems the most important quality young men and women rave about these days is, "He's hot!" or "She's hot!" Now, I am all for physical chemistry. I certainly felt a chemistry draw me toward Rob, but it can't be the only quality. Sex is great, and should be a high priority in a marriage, but marriage is far more than sex. My children laugh at my acronym for HOT:

Holy
Obedient to God
Totally following God's plan

"Laugh all you want," I smile. "You'll see that I am right!"

Joining together as man and wife in prayer is powerful. Joining together with your children during family devotions and praying for your marriage that allows them to witness your covenant as a "cord of three strands" (Ecclesiastes 4:12). Hearing your mate assure you that he is praying for you builds a deep sense of security and trust—and vice versa.

Fifth, and finally, halt harsh communication. I am going to stand on the shoulders of marital relations giants Dan B. Allender and Tremper Longman.

> Bad talk attacks, blames and dismisses the other with contempt. Contempt is a belittling of the other, of their words or motives. All effort to make the other person small is an attempt to make yourself big, powerful and in control. Any time you huff and puff and try to blow the other down, you are operating in contempt. Contempt shows itself in the tone, the eyes and the content of a conversation. Whenever it shows up, true talk is done. It is pointless and in fact harmful to proceed once the cancer of contempt shows itself. It must be named and transformed before the conversation has any hope of becoming intimate truth.[8]

Now, I am not a marriage expert, but I've been married long enough to know that speaking harshly to my husband gets me nowhere. It is a dead-end street. Harsh communication is like poison in a relationship, quickly eroding my deep friendship with Rob. It shuts him down.

Scientists agree that "marital difficulties are often a source of chronic stress. Bickering may have long-term consequences for overall health status."[9] They have found that "low quality marriages exhibit an even greater health risk than do divorced individuals."[10]

And be sure to deal with underlying issues. Don't sweep things under the rug. Let me repeat myself: don't sweep things under the rug! In five years you'll have Mount Everest in your living room. Secret, underlying issues that go unchecked grow into huge, often insurmountable, obstacles. If you need counseling, get it. I admit, I have had to get counseling at certain periods of my emotional healing, and I am glad I did. Counseling and accountability were the gentle hands that led me to experience emotional health and well-being for the first time in my life. None of us is perfect; therefore, there will be times we need to deal with some issue of our sin nature. I suggest praying together, on a daily basis, finding an accountability partner or seeking counsel as needed.

Dr. John Gottman coined "The Four Horsemen" of poor communication. Do you recognize any of these? Are some or all of these horses in your barn? (Smile!) I think I have ridden each of these four horses:

- **Criticism:** Complaints are normal, but criticism deals more with your spouse's character and personality.
- **Contempt:** This is long-simmering negative thoughts about your partner that turn into disrespect.
- **Defensiveness:** This approach rarely works and usually turns the conversation into a blame game.
- **Stonewalling:** Eventually your partner tunes you out.[11]

Ugh. I am a master at each of these. It has taken years to overcome negative communication. Years to learn the art of healthy communication. But, I am here to assure you it can be done. And I promise that once you have tasted the fruit of healthy relationships, you will never return to dysfunction. It will not be welcome in your house. We will dig deeper into the importance of healthy communication patterns in chapter 10: "Training the Tongue." As for now, begin afresh today. Remember, "Today is fresh, but tomorrow will be fresher!" Let God do a new thing in your marriage. Let him restore your marriage and make it even better than you can imagine.

Time in the Tower

Today Is Fresh, but Tomorrow Will Be Fresher!

1. Dr. Archibald Hart writes, "We were created for relationships. Everything about us was designed to live in close community and interaction with others. We certainly were not designed to go through life emotionally disconnected."[12] Do you agree or disagree with this statement? Is there any part of you that feels "emotionally disconnected" with your spouse today? If so, take time to pray about reconnecting. Take one active step toward reconnecting.

2. Jay Kesler writes, "Think back to the earliest stages of courtship when you fell in love and couldn't stand being apart. You spent hours talking or just being together enjoying one another's presence."[13] How is this possible when you have three screaming children clinging to you? Where in the world do you find the energy, stamina, and charisma to have a viable relationship with your mate?

3. Think of ways to keep "the fire in the fireplace"—i.e., the romance in your relationship.

4. An acrostic for "FRESH" was given in this chapter. It spoke of five principles that could help make your marriage fresher. Did any of these stand out to you? If so, which one(s)? Consider and outline the strengths and weaknesses of your marriage.

Marital Weaknesses	Marital Strengths

Now write down five things that could help make your marriage fresher.

Notes

1. Dr. Archibald Hart and Dr. Sharon Hart Morris, *Safe Haven Marriage: Building a Relationship You Want to Come Home To* (Nashville: W Publishing Group, 2006), 50.

2. Jay Kesler, *Raising Responsible Kids: Ten Things You Can Do Now to Prepare Your Child for a Lifetime of Independence* (Brentwood, TN: Wolgemuth & Hyatt, 1991), 13–15.

3. Sinclair Ferguson, *Let's Study Philippians* (Carlisle, PA: Banner of Truth, 1997), 109.

4. Michael Farris, *A Sacred Foundation: The Importance of Strength in the Home School Marriage* (Sisters, OR: Loyal Publishing, 2000), 183.

5. Dr. John Gottman, "The Science of a Good Marriage—friendship between couples is a key to good marital foundation," http://www.findarticles.com.

6. Noah Webster, *An American Dictionary of the English Language* (New York: S. Converse, 1828). Facsimile first edition (Chesapeake, VA: Foundation for American Christian Education, 1967 and all subsequent editions).

7. Gary Thomas, *A Sacred Marriage* (Grand Rapids, MI: Zondervan, 2000), 13.

8. Dan Allender and Tremper Longman, *The Intimate Mystery: Creating Strength and Beauty in Your Marriage* (Westmont, IL: InterVarsity, 2005), 62.

9. Andrew Herrmann, "Kiss and Make up: A Bad Marriage Could Make You Ill," *Chicago Sun Times*, http://www.findarticles.com/p/articles/mi_qn4155/is_20060327/ai_n16175926.

10. Ibid.

11. Dr. John Gottman, *Why Marriages Succeed or Fail: And How You Can Make Yours Last* (New York: Fireside, 1994), 72.

12. Dr. Archibald Hart and Dr. Sharon Hart Morris, *Safe Haven Marriage: Building a Relationship You Want to Come Home To*, 50.

13. Jay Kesler, *Raising Responsible Kids: Ten Things You Can Do Now to Prepare Your Child for a Lifetime of Independence*, 14.

DEVOTION
Thirty Minutes of Silence

evotion, defined as "a solemn attention to the Supreme Being in worship; a yielding of the heart and the affections to God,"[1] should be the first priority of the day. From the youngest to the oldest in our homes, we can, through much training and repetition, inaugurate "thirty minutes of silence" in our daily routine.

"Impossible," you say. "This will never happen. You don't know my family!"

You are right. I don't know your family. But, I know mine. And if we can do this, I have no doubt in my mind you can do it. After all, "Nothing is impossible with God" (Luke 1:37). Here are a few suggestions.

1. Lay the groundwork.

Your children may ask over and over again (like mine did), "Why do we need a quiet time?" They need to know why you are enforcing this new discipline. Begin by reading the biblical accounts of Jesus' devotional life, explaining the "why's" behind the discipline of living this way. Luke shows us this in Luke 5:16: "But Jesus often withdrew to lonely places and prayed." Luke's choice of the word *often* makes it crystal clear that Jesus had a regular habit of retreating from the crowds that buffeted him daily. He needed to recharge. He needed to connect with his Father. We don't have throngs of people racing after us, but we do have our own pressures. Just like Jesus, we need to find a solitary place. Take a few minutes and read his story with your family. Notice the simple choices he made:

- A boat (Matthew 14:13)
- A lake (Mark 3:7)
- A town called Bethsaida (Luke 9:10)
- A garden (John 18:1, KJV)
- A mountain (John 6:15)
- A desert (John 11:54)

2. Start slowly.

Begin by setting apart five or ten minutes in a place where the house is quiet—no mechanical devices. Turn the answering machine volume off—no talking and no interaction—everyone in their room or space, and quiet. Wean your family off noise and get them practicing a period of silence.

3. Be consistent.

Training requires repetition and consistency. Eventually, and I emphasize *eventually*, it will be something they look forward to. One initial reason we chose to homeschool our three children was to bond as a family. After many years, my oldest and I began to chuckle, "We've got way too much bonding (affectionately known as "TMB!") going on here. We need some space from one another." Quiet time became a sacred refuge, a time when we retreated to our rooms and recharged.

4. Eliminate static.

Static is defined as "noise produced in a radio or television receiver by atmospheric or other electrical disturbances."[2] Spend a few moments evaluating the present "static" in your family life. Is the television constantly on? If so, why? At least mute the commercials. What about emotional static? This type of static is described as "criticism, opposition, or unwanted interference by somebody else."[3] We will talk more about this in chapter 10, "Training the Tongue," but for now, minimize emotional static by minding your own business. If the phone rings, my daughter, Brooke, immediately has to know who is on the phone. Simple, ordinary actions can drain energy. Be on the lookout.

5. Pinpoint distractions.

Distraction wears many faces: solicitors, telephone calls, knocks at the door, projects, television programs, etc. Proverbs 4:25 has proven a wonderful antidote for this problem: "Let your eyes look straight ahead, fix your gaze directly before you."

What task lies in front of you right now? A sink full of dirty dishes? A child who is crying out for attention? Preparation for dinner? A job opportunity? An aging parent? If so, don't accept a friend's phone call, *unless it is a real emergency*! Call her back when you have time to chat. Easy? No. I didn't say it would be. But, when I fix my gaze on that which is right in front of me, I am able to stay focused and can defeat the distraction.

One of my greatest personal struggles has been delaying my own personal gratification by saying no to certain opportunities that would distract me from focused parenting. Recently, I wanted to attend an October writer's conference in New Mexico in order to meet with editors who might publish my first book. Initially, my husband and I thought we could make it work, but as the deadline for registration came closer, we looked over our schedules and realized it would be a great strain on our family if I left town.

"Can you please wait, Janell? I hate to ask you to delay this, but it would really help us out if you didn't leave town right now," requested my husband.

Once again, I had to adjust my focus and lay down my own desires. Of course, I pouted for a while. But, somehow, deep down inside, I knew God saw my heart and would accomplish his will when the timing was right.

And recently, in one week, I was asked to start a new children's missions program at my church, teach middle school English at a local Christian school, and serve as publicity chairman (again) for my local churches' women's retreat. Each offer produced great angst in my heart, because I would have loved to do each thing—but accepting these positions would have blurred my vision and sidetracked me from my true calling, which at the time was managing my household and finishing the race with my two high schoolers, Brooke and Grant. Not all doors of opportunities are meant to be walked through; some must be closed (and perhaps opened later) and others locked tightly (never to be opened again).

6. *Identify stressors.*

Disturbance is an "interruption of a settled state of things; disorder; any disquiet or interruption of peace."[4] Well, any mother of young children will respond with a loud, resounding, "Yes! My life is one big disturbance!" How many times a day, or even an hour, are there interruptions of peace? This is to be expected, and often welcomed, but what other areas of your home or lives are causing unnecessary interruptions of peace? Can you identify what is causing emotional stress?

Rushing causes me great distress—it interrupts my peace. I used to be able to hurry and scurry my way through the day, but no more. Perhaps it is age or perhaps it is physical limitations, but I can't do rushing. I agree with Kirk Byron Jones, who writes, "Spirituality rarely involves rushing. Spirituality is courted by attentiveness."[5]

Jones says to do away with rushing by implementing the "savoring pace."[6] I call it "living a *now* life." The here and *now.* Remember the power that exists in that three-letter word? When the lightbulb went off in my brain concerning "living a now life," my black-and-white world of hurry, worry, and scurry transformed into full Technicolor. It was absolutely freeing. For once in my life, I wasn't living in the next day or the next month. I was living in the moment.

One very special day, my daughter and I had the opportunity to show up for life. While attending a conference, we stopped life for a few moments to order dessert. It had been a long, arduous day for her, so I thought she deserved a special treat. She ordered a root beer float—an $8.00 root beer float. (*This ought to be something*, I thought.) When it arrived, it lived up to its billing. Arranged beautifully on a big, white plate was a large, decorative glass containing five scoops of creamy vanilla ice cream, a bottle of famous IBC root beer, and three delectable chocolate chip cookies. Her eyes were big as saucers and mine even bigger!

I couldn't help but delight in the beautiful presentation of this dessert. I raved about it to the waitress as she poured the chilled root beer over the vanilla ice cream, transforming simple ingredients into a volcanic float!

"Janell, what's the big deal?" my friend called from the opposite end of the table. "It's a root beer float!"

"Yes, indeed, it is," I smiled, "perhaps the prettiest one I've ever seen." For just a moment, I savored life. And I enjoyed the show. Is it so terrible to take the time to enjoy the ordinary blessings of ordinary life? I don't think so. (And my daughter certainly didn't think so!)

7. *Identify chaos and confusion.*

What areas of life seem to cause chaos? A disorganized kitchen? Potty training? Grocery shopping with the children? Mismanaged time? An overwhelming laundry load? Poor eating habits? Work schedules? Telephone conversations? Extracurricular activity overload?

Pinpoint these areas and be proactive in doing something to rectify the situation. For example, with three children under the age of four, including twins, I found household cleaning very difficult. The greatest gift my husband ever gave me was hiring someone to clean my house. Even on our modest income, he made a way to afford this much-needed assistance.

My friend, Sandy, is a homeschooling mother of six. The greatest gift her husband, Eric, ever gave her was a college-age woman to assist her two days a week. Her helping hands freed Sandy to work with the older children on their more difficult subjects while the nanny attended to the younger children. A simple solution that gave great rewards.

Don't quit. This journey toward training your families in this discipline can be laborious and wearisome. Please, take courage and persevere. I can attest to the fact that the path can and will be arduous, but the rewards will be sweet.

8. *Learn to rest.*

Last, but not least, remember that God, our Creator, took the time to rest. After creating the entire universe, which must have taken quite a bit of energy, God decided to implement the principle of rest. Setting the example for all time, he rested, enjoying the fruit of his labor. Sally Breedlove tells us, "From God's point of view, rest is not an accessory blessing. Our lives are meant to flow from a solid garden core of spacious inner quiet. When we turn to the Creation story we see how foundational rest is."[7]

Solomon instructs, "By wisdom a house is built, and through understanding it is established; through knowledge its rooms are filled with rare and beautiful treasures" (Proverbs 24:3–4). God desires our homes to be full of pleasant and precious riches. Riches, as spoken of here, refer to an abundance of spiritual blessings. On my morning walk, I pass many homes, praying for the families as I go. As my walk comes to a close and I am in front of my own home, I stop for a second and transform Proverbs 24:3–4 into a personal prayer over my family. It goes something like this:

Dear Lord, this is my home. Within the walls of this precious place are my husband and three children. And, Abraham, my dog, too. I pray that each and every room will be filled with the riches of your presence, your grace, your love, your power, and your serenity. May wisdom, knowledge, and understanding guide us through this day. Help me, today, to be a drink of fresh water for my family.

Thank you, Lord, for such a wonderful family.

Serenity of soul is one of those rare and beautiful treasures. A person who removes tension from the air, who operates in serenity of soul, is like a fresh breeze blowing off the ocean. It only takes one person to change the spiritual atmosphere of a home. Don't you agree?

While stealing some "alone" time in Bermuda, my husband and I spent eight days in a cabana that jutted out over the crystal clear, sparkling blue water of the Atlantic Ocean. No air-conditioning. No screens on the windows. Only the fresh ocean breezes to keep us cool. Upon arriving at this cabana, I thought to myself, "You have to be kidding me. No way. Eight days without air-conditioning? Rob didn't say we were going camping in Bermuda. What in the world was he thinking?"

But that night, when the negative ions of the Atlantic Ocean permeated our room, I slept more soundly than I had in a very long time. Now, I am not a scientist, but I do know there is something pretty spectacular about ocean air. Denise Mann confirms:

There's something in the air and while it may not be love, some say it's the next best thing—negative ions. Negative ions are odorless, tasteless, and invisible molecules that we inhale in abundance in certain environments. Think mountains, waterfalls, and beaches. Once they reach our bloodstream, negative ions are believed to produce biochemical

reactions that increase levels of the mood chemical sero-
tonin, helping to alleviate depression, relieve stress, and boost
our daytime energy. For a whopping one in three of us who
are sensitive to their effects, negative ions can make us feel
like we are walking on air.[8]

The air that circulates in the mountains and at the beach is
said to "contain tens of thousands of negative ions—much more
than the average home or office building, which contain dozens
or hundreds, and many register a flat zero."[9] So, as you develop
the devotional state of your family, ask yourself a few questions:

- Is my home registering a flat zero in the serenity category?
- Is the spiritual air in my home full of "negative ion" energy?
  Encouragement? Laughter? Joy? Love? Faith? Or is the spiritual air in my home full of "positive ion" energy? Con-
  tention? Strife? Anger? Impatience? Frustration?
- Are we moving through life with more serenity than irritation? Not just on a good day—every day.
- On a typical day, do I read the Bible? Have devotions? Talk
  to my children about God?
- Is my soul running on empty, with nothing left to give? Is it
  overloaded with care and concern for others?

These are necessary questions. How can we serve our families, churches, and communities if we are empty? I faced this
question with great care and knew I needed to withdraw for a
season in order to find the answer. Responsibilities compound,
obligations mount, and all of a sudden we find ourselves in the
midst of the whirlwind, drained of any positive emotion. Why?
Because in the midst of the whirlwind, we forget to take care of
ourselves and our relationship to God.

Having always been a disciplined individual, I'd never dis-
missed my quiet time with God, but the deeper disciplines of

practiced silence, journaling, and meditation had lain dormant. Honestly, I was too tired, too run-down, and too burned out to even consider these options. Then, I read a powerful Scripture verse, Revelation 8:1: "When he opened the seventh seal, there was silence in heaven for about half an hour."

Silence for half an hour. Thirty minutes. After the September 11, 2001, tragedy at the World Trade Center in New York City, "moments of silence" were being held throughout the world. One such memoriam was held at the New York Stock Exchange. This time the silence was for two minutes. I remember watching as this usually hectic, hustling world marketplace was silent. It seemed like forever. Absolutely no noise or movement. It was profound.

I couldn't help but reflect on Revelation 8:1 and the intensity of this silence. Matthew Henry comments, "Great things were upon the wheel of providence, and the church of God, both in heaven and earth, stood silent, as became them, to see what God was doing."[10]

"There has been a great effort among commentators to interpret the meaning of this silence. I think that it is a hush of awe before the march of the awful judgments about to come, the calm before the storm breaks forth, the oppressive silence before the burst of battle. It is designed to emphasize the events that follow."[11]

This compelling thought moved me deeply and provoked me to implement this practice in my daily life, in order to restore my relationship to Jesus and be that one person in my household who infuses serenity and creates sanctuary. I understand, at least I try to understand, the gravity of the situation recorded in Revelation 8:1. In no way am I comparing my personal struggle to the opening of the seventh seal—I am merely saying that God's declaration of a thirty-minute time of silence is evidence that we, too, would do well to embrace a period of silence in our daily lives—especially when things are difficult. Heaven apparently deemed this principle important, so I decided I must integrate this practice into my daily life. Over the course of several months, I trained myself, with God's immeasurable help, to experience a full thirty minutes of silence. It took me a long time to slow down the pace of my life, but beginning each day with five or ten minutes of complete silence in the confines of my closet, I slowly saw the cares, demands, pressures, and drivenness of my soul dissipate. And I emerged from this time of communion with God stronger, wiser, and better equipped to handle the whirlwind our households often become.

Music lessons, dance lessons, soccer games, birthday parties, Girl Scouts, Boy Scouts, church youth group, etc. The list goes on and on. While these are all good things, are they the best things? Herein lies the challenge: Are we moving through life with more serenity than irritation? Or are all these wonderful, exhilarating activities and opportunities robbing us of a quality life and enriched family time? Are they infusing our homes with deep satisfaction and rich relationships? Or are they crowding an already busy household?

Now that we've laid the groundwork for establishing thirty minutes of silence in our homes and lives, let's take a look at developing the devotional life of our family. First and foremost, inaugurate family devotions.

My husband and I began this practice when Candace was seven and our twins were three. Full of wiggle and giggle, they did their best to be still. Initially, we would say short sentence prayers and off to bed they went. As they grew older, our time of prayer lengthened a bit, we added a devotional thought or teaching, and we spent time at the close of our hectic days recognizing God and one another. It's been a daily habit in our family for more than thirteen years now. Nothing extraordinary, but vital to the spiritual health of our home. With Candace in college, prayers are often via the phone, but nonetheless, we pray together.

Anne Ortlund, author of *Children Are Wet Cement*, shares: "It seems to me most families fall off the horse one way or the other: they don't have any family worship at all, or they make it such a big deal, it's oppressive." She writes,

> "Short Children, Short Devotions; Longer Children, Longer Devotions."[12]

"I appreciate Daddy Ray's rule: Short children, short devotions; longer children, longer devotions." When our first three were very tiny, we read no Scripture at all. We told a short, vivid Bible story with plenty of action in it and had a little prayer. Or we sang an action song about Jesus. Or we mentioned a short verse. But we didn't do all these every day. As they grew, we read a little simple Scripture. Or we shared a little of how the Lord had helped us in our lives that day. Or we sang a hymn together, or memorized a verse. Sometimes Ray prayed, sometimes Mother, sometimes a child; only on a leisurely morning did we all pray. In the beginning, we led our children sentence by sentence, to teach them to pray. Later sometimes we said the Lord's Prayer in unison as a family. We usually ended at the first sign of restlessness.[13]

Her wise counsel offers many different ways to approach family devotions and demonstrates once again how very simple it really is. No bells and whistles, no hoopla, just a consistent—there's that word again—gathering together as a family to take our concerns to a great, big God who knows more than we do. I offer no formula for success, only an admonition to begin. Just start and have fun with it.

This consistent practice will provide the spiritual atmosphere for leading our children to Christ. Mark 10:13–16 reads, "People were bringing little children to Jesus to have him touch them, but the disciples rebuked them. When Jesus saw this, he was indignant. He said to them, 'Let the little children come to me, and do not hinder them, for the kingdom of God belongs to such as these. I tell you the truth, anyone who will not receive the kingdom of God like a little child will never enter it.' And he took the children in his arms, put his hands on them and blessed them."

This is the most important aspect of establishing a devotional life in our families—leading our children to Christ. I didn't think it was possible, until one day, my little three-and-a-half-year-old, Candace, bowed her head and asked Jesus to be her Lord and Savior. My husband and I had been reading from and discussing Kenneth N. Taylor's *The Bible in Pictures for Little Eyes*, which I highly recommend, and lo and behold, after reading about the three crosses and the thief (see Luke 23: 32–43), she asked that we pray with her "to ask Jesus into her heart." Obviously, the seeds that had been planted the first three and a half years were about to sprout.

Brooke and Grant, on the other hand, were five. After a teaching series on the book of Daniel they both wanted to know the "one true God" that Daniel knew. It was a great evening. Even though my children were at different ages, the spiritual climate was exactly the same. They were being taught the Word of God. We are promised in Isaiah 55:10–11, "As the rain and the snow come down from heaven, and do not return to it without watering the earth and making it bud and flourish, so that it yields seed for the sower and bread for the eater, so is my word that goes out from my mouth: It will not return to me empty, but will accomplish what I desire and achieve the purpose for which I sent it."

George Barna writes,

> Part of my responsibility as a parent and as a member of the community of faith is to expose young children to the his-

tory, the expectations and the ways of God. During the formative years, children develop their decision-making perspectives and patterns. Helping them in that process is one of the most important responsibilities we have as humans; engaging them at a young age is a critical strategic choice. In order for our children to grow into whole and healthy people, we must help them build strong foundations to prepare them for the rest of their lives. Because everything is ultimately a spiritual and moral issue, the more intentional and clear minded we are regarding their spiritual development, the better off they will be for the duration of their lives.[14]

We must bathe our children's lives in prayer and receive God's vision for each one. " 'For I know the plans I have for you,' declares the LORD, 'plans to prosper you and not to harm you, plans to give you hope and a future. Then you will call upon me and come and pray to me, and I will listen to you. You will seek me and find me when you seek me with all your heart. I will be found by you,' declares the LORD" (Jeremiah 29:11–14).

God has a plan for each child. With a watchful eye and a listening ear, we begin to understand it. As I watched Candace in her early years, I saw that music was very important to her. So, I surrounded her little soul with beautiful worship music. Long, weary nights up with perpetual ear infections led me to play worship music to soothe her. It did seem to calm her. During the day, we would dance around the house, laughing and being crazy. But, her favorite event was our "Concert of Peace," held occasionally at bedtime.

My journal records one special night:

Friday night, I had the beautiful privilege of giving my daughter yet another "Concert of Peace." Our usual nighttime ritual consists of putting on jammies, reading a book, and lying down together. Usually Daddy carries out the duties, but tonight Daddy was very weary in well doing. So, Mommy would do it tonight. Together, we lay upon her bed, snuggled deep in the warm blanket—relaxed and peaceful. Instead of reading a book, I suggested singing songs. We started with 'Jesus Loves Me.' After applauding this quiet chorus, she began her requests: *Grapes. Red. Running Over. Green Grapes.* She had little thoughts and wanted me to make up songs about each one. Now, who said motherhood wasn't a difficult task? An intellectual position? Not everyone can write songs about green grapes on the spur of the moment! After each little chorus, a smile would emerge on her little face and applause rang. Her applause resounded in my ears and echoed in my heart. The concert closed with her favorite night-night song, written especially for her, and sung to her since birth:

> 'Go to sleep, my little child.
> Close your eyes in peace.
> Drift away to Heaven's gates,
> Angels are guarding thee.'

I realized right then and there that while some strive for fame, others for appearances before great crowds, nothing compares to the beauty of singing a child to sleep. Seeing the reward of a peaceful countenance and a secure heart far outweighs the applause of any audience anywhere.

Who would have known that Candace, as a young woman, would excel at the piano, passionately writing worship songs that both pierce the heart and calm the soul?

As you observe your own children daily, you will begin to see (if you haven't already) little signs that point to God's purpose. Pray over these things, pay attention to them, and create the necessary environment for them to develop.

In the chart "Developing Devotionals Using the Q.U.I.E.T. Method" in the Appendix, I offer five simple principles for creating a devotional life in your family:

- *Questions* are a terrific way to draw your child into vivid discussions about God throughout your daily routine (Deuteronomy 6:4–9).
- *Unlock* the mysteries of God. Openly discuss the profound mysteries of God's amazing world (Mark 4:10–11).
- *Inspire* at every opportunity! Always be on the lookout for the little lessons tucked away in life. Lessons will rouse the interest (Psalm 100, MSG).
- *Enlarge* each child's understanding of God through hands-on learning activities. Activate the five senses. One of the simplest, yet most rewarding, things we ever did was invest in a simple butterfly farm. What an amazing sight to behold! Watching little caterpillars spin their cocoons, hang upside down for days and days, and then struggle to emerge as butterflies was money well spent. The process of metamorphosis engaged my children and fostered many questions and spiritual discussions: Why is the caterpillar hanging upside down? Is it dead? Why is there blood coming out of the cocoon? Enthralled by their observation and discovery, their little minds whirled with curiosity and inquiry. They grasped the spiritual teachings of regeneration and conversion (Psalm 92:1–5).
- *Testify* to God's working in your own quiet time. Talk about your private devotions. Make God very real to your children (1 John 4:13–15).

And, finally, plug into the power of the Holy Spirit. Romans 15:13 says, "May the God of hope fill you with all joy and peace as you trust in him, so that you may overflow with hope by the power of the Holy Spirit." Overflow. That's the beauty of living a devotional life. When time is set apart for the infilling of God's Spirit, on a consistent basis, the end result is overflow. No longer deprived of necessary spiritual "negative ions," which recharge and replenish, true spirituality will spill over and fill each and every room of your home with rare and beautiful treasures.

Time in the Tower

Thirty Minutes of Silence

1. As parents, we have to ask questions:

   - Are we moving through life with more serenity than irritation?
   - Or are all these wonderful, exhilarating activities and opportunities robbing us of a quality life and enriched family time?
   - Are these activities infusing our homes with deep satisfaction and rich relationships?
   - Or are they crowding an already busy household?

   Take a few moments to consider your answers. Can you think of small ways in which you can begin to implement the suggested "thirty minutes of silence" into your daily routine?

2. Using the chart "Developing Devotionals Using the Q.U.I.E.T. Method" in the Appendix, begin laying the groundwork for a family devotional time. Listed below are several resources:
   http://www.wholesomewords.org/family/famaltar.html
   http://www.cefonline.com/
   http://www.childrensministry.com/

Notes

1. Noah Webster, *An American Dictionary of the English Language* (New York: S. Converse, 1828). Facsimile first edition (Chesapeake, VA: Foundation for American Christian Education, 1967 and all subsequent editions).

2. Ibid.

3. Encarta Dictionary, http://encarta.msn.com/dictionary_/static.html.

4. Noah Webster, *An American Dictionary of the English Language*.

5. Kirk Byron Jones, *Addicted to Hurry* (Valley Forge: Judson Press, 2003), 15.

6. Ibid., 67.

7. Sally Breedlove, *Choosing Rest: Cultivating a Sunday Heart in a Monday World* (Colorado Springs: NavPress, 2002), 24.

8. Denise Mann, "Negative Ions Create Positive Vibes," *Green Home Environmental Store*, http://www.greenhome.com/info/articles/the_air_we_breathe/127/, 1.

9. Ibid., 2.

10. Matthew Henry, *Acts to Revelation [Matthew Henry's Commentary on the Whole Bible, vol. VI]* (MacClean, VA: MacDonald Publishing Company, n.d.), 1150.

11. B.W. Johnson, "The Revelation of John," *The People's New Testament*, http://www.ccel.org/j/johnson_bw/pnt/PNT27-08.htm.

12. Anne Ortlund, *Children are Wet Cement* (Grand Rapids: Revell Books, 1981), 80.

13. Ibid.

14. George Barna, *Transforming Children into Spiritual Champions: Why Children Should Be Your Church's #1 Priority* (Ventura, CA: Regal Books, 2003), 32.

PRAYER
"He Simply Prayed"

> "Prayer lays hold of God's plan and becomes the link between His will and its accomplishment on earth. Amazing things happen, and we are given the privilege of being the channels of the Holy Spirit's prayer."[1]

Late one stormy night, my doorbell rang. There at the door stood my dear friend, Sherri, soaked to the bone. "He's gone. He left me for another woman. He said he never loved me."

I welcomed her in, embraced her shaking body, and wrapped her in a warm blanket. "Let me make you a cup of hot tea, Sherri," I said softly.

Sherri's entire world was coming to an abrupt end that stormy night. Her ideal Christian marriage was now a stark statistic. She now faced raising three small children alone. "What in the world am I going to do?" she cried.

"I don't know the answer, Sherri, but I do know the One who holds your heart in his hand. First things first—let's pray."

Prayer is an intangible, something we can't quite grasp with our hands. *Intangible* meaning, "Nonmaterial, without material qualities, and so not able to be touched or seen."[2] We can interpret prayer as "hard to describe, difficult to define or describe clearly, but nonetheless perceived."[3] Perhaps the traditional folding of the hands or holding someone else's hand in prayer helps us feel as though we are actually holding on to something. Prayer can seem futile at times and provokes questions, such as:

"Are my prayers going beyond the ceiling of my living room?"

"Does God even listen?"

"Does it really make a difference?"

"Is God real?"

"What's the use?"

"Why spend good time doing something so surreal—dreamlike and strange?"

A cloud of mystery often surrounds prayer, but in its simplest form, prayer is merely conversing with God—talking to him and listening to him. Prayer, the intangible act, produces answers, the tangible results. There is no doubt in my mind that God answers prayer. I've seen him do it over and over again. Sherri and I prayed day by day, minute by minute, for God's help, God's restoration, and God's mercy over her situation. We prayed for finances, emo-

> Prayer, the intangible act, produces answers, the tangible results.

tional strength and healing, spiritual mentors for her children, patience and understanding, wisdom, and much more. Today, years later, she is a living testimony to the faithfulness of God. Even during her recent battle with advanced breast cancer, she transformed her own private pain into a ministry of intercession for others. Ever the encourager, she told me, "One thing I have noticed about adversity, and this is certainly related to prayer, it is as if God is saying, 'Come a little closer.' It is the sweet with the bitter."

Sherri is right. In prayer, we come a little closer to God. In my life, prayer is spiritual oxygen. Without it, I can't breathe. And I am completely convinced my family couldn't survive without it. As I draw closer to God, the air is purer, fresher, and more invigorating. On a regular basis, before my husband leaves for work, he prays for my day, the children's day, and our home. Some days it is only a few very short sentences.

"Lord, help Janell. Give her strength. Watch over the household."

Nothing remarkable to the naked eye, but deep in my soul a supernatural sense of rest and peace settles over me after he prays. Why? Because we have placed the order of our day in God's hands. The atmosphere of our home changes and we all breathe a little easier. "Praying in humble dependence indicates that we are genuinely convinced of God's wisdom, love, goodness, and power," writes Wayne Grudem. "When we truly pray, we as persons, in the wholeness of our character, are relating to God as a person, in the wholeness of his character. Thus, all we think or feel about God comes to expression in our prayer."[4] Since childhood, I have depended on God, talking to him as if he were right next to me. This simple practice has led me on a lifelong quest to know more about prayer.

After years of hungering for this truth, I have found no better dissertation on the subject of prayer than the words of Andrew Murray, a nineteenth-century South African revivalist, penned in *Raising Your Children for Christ*. Murray's family emigrated from Scotland to South Africa, where his father was pastor to a church. Andrew was born into a godly home where prayer was normal and hymns were sung around the house. Most of all, Andrew's father prayed for revival. Every Friday evening he would read to his family accounts of the great movings of the Holy Spirit in history. Then he would go to his study and with tears pour out his heart to God for a similar outpouring on South Africa. Those experiences marked young Andrew deeply. He grew up and became a pastor and writer, whose work we glean from today.

In Judges 13:12 Manoah, Samson's father, prays, "When your words are fulfilled, what is to be the rule for the boy's life and work?" Here is where it all starts—asking God for "the rule" concerning our children's lives and work. Murray's keen insight into Manoah's petition to God concerning the raising of Samson leads us to several significant truths, and bears repeating:

1. Manoah immediately prayed.

At once, Manoah turned to God for the answer. Obviously, he didn't pick up a phone. He didn't read a book. He didn't go for counsel. Today those are all good things, but first he went to the throne of God on behalf of his son. True success comes when we kneel before God and ask him to reveal his plan and purpose for our children.

Under the divine oversight of God himself, our children were formed. He is the Author of their being. His hands held them. His breath gave them their first breath. His eyes beheld their potential and promise. His face shone heaven's peace all around them. His heart swelled with pride over the work of his hands. He saw that his creation was *very good*. Psalm 139:13–16 tells us: "For you created my inmost being; you knit me together in my mother's womb. I praise you because I am fearfully and wonderfully made; your works are wonderful, I know that full well. My frame was not hidden from you when I was made in the secret place. When I was woven together in the depths of the earth, your eyes saw my unformed body. All the days ordained for me were written in your book before one of them came to be."

When I stop to consider that each of my three children is uniquely designed, fashioned, and formed by the King of kings,

"Manoah's sense of need immediately found expression in prayer. He believed in God as the living God, as the hearer of prayer. He believed that when God gave a command or a task, he would also give the grace to do it right. He believed that when God gave a child to be trained for his service, he would also give the wisdom needed to do so. Instead of the sense of unfitness and weakness depressing him, or the sense of his obligation causing him to work in his own strength, he simply prayed. Prayer to Manoah was the solution to difficulties, the supply of need, the source of wisdom and strength."[5]

I become humble and quiet. He saw fit to trust me with them and knows it is my job to develop the creative potential he placed in them. You and I are called to shape our children into all God intended.

Manoah understood this important truth. That's why he asked God to show him the rule and work of Samson's life. On a daily basis, I am doing the same—asking God to show me the rule and work of my three children's lives. Here's an idea of this week's prayers:

What is the rule and work for . . . ?	Prayer for week of _____
Candace	Direction for Summer Internships: Lord, where do you want Candace? Boston? New York? Home? You know her future and her station in life. Put her where she will be equipped. Trained. Readied.

(Continued)

What is the rule and work for . . . ?	Prayer for week of _____
Brooke	Healing. Restore Brooke totally. She has been very sick. Give her the strength to do her schoolwork with excellence. Help her overcome her dyslexia day by day. Guide every activity and opportunity so Brooke will be prepared to enter college next year. Lead her to the college of YOUR choosing.
Grant	Grant is on the threshold of leaving the haven of home to venture off to college. Where will that be? Direct his search and open doors that only you can open. Will he play soccer in college? He's mentioned majoring in Christian Education and minoring in coaching. Lord, solidify that calling.

It is quite a responsibility, I know, but one he has ordained for us to carry. Aren't you glad God is our Enabler and our Strength? Remember, we don't have to do this job alone (Psalm 46:1).

As I write these words, I remember an encounter I had with a sweet little girl in Wal-Mart. I struck up a conversation with her while we waited in line. She showed me a *Rugrats* video and asked, "Do your children watch this movie?"

How does she know I have children? I thought. I gently answered, "No, they do not. *Rugrats* are really noisy and I don't like the way they treat one another."

She thought a minute, looked up at me, and asked quizzically, "Do you beat your daughters?"

Once again, I thought, *How does she know I have daughters?* Stunned, I repeated her question. "What did you say? Do I beat my daughters?" Shaken by her question, I whispered, "Well, no, I don't. Do you get beaten?" Her mother was involved with the cashier and had no idea of what her daughter was saying to me.

I prayed.

"No, I not bad," she whispered in her cute little four-year-old voice, "I be good."

I asked her name and she asked mine. I proceeded to tell her that my name, Janell, means, "God's gracious gift." I told her I was a gift to my parents and that I thought she was a special gift as well.

Suddenly, we were interrupted and that was the end of my conversation with this preschooler. I couldn't get her off my mind, as I wondered what impressions were being made on her young heart. I prayed a hedge of protection around her, asking the Lord to intervene and continue placing godly people in her path.

This one encounter serves as a reminder that the early years of life are paramount to the success of a child's development. "Timing is everything," writes Dr. Bruce D. Perry, MD, PhD. "Bonding experiences lead to healthy attachments and healthy attachment capabilities when they are provided in the earliest years of life. During the first three years of life, the human brain develops to 90% of adult size and puts in place the majority of systems and structures that will be responsible for all future emotional, behavioral, social, and physiological functioning during the rest of life."[6]

> "Very often, the multitude of professional voices drown out the voice of God. We become so dependent on what they say we should do that the simplicity of God's Word seems insufficient."

Manoah didn't have the advantage of Dr. Perry's sage advice, as we do, but he instinctively knew the power and importance of laying a strong foundation in Samson's early life. Manoah was a man ahead of his time. He set the example that generation upon generation would follow. Somehow, I'm envious of Manoah. He lived in a simpler time. No cable channels. No Doctor Phil. No Oprah. No libraries full of self-help books. No parenting guides. No, Manoah had one resource: God Almighty. Therefore, he depended solely on God's help to raise his son. Very often, the multitude of professional voices, like the ones mentioned above, drown out the voice of God. We become so dependent on what they say we should do that the simplicity of God's Word seems insufficient. Manoah knew better. He knew God was trustworthy and sufficient.

2. Manoah believed in God as the hearer of prayer.[8]

"The Sovereign LORD has given me an instructed tongue, to know the word that sustains the weary. He wakens me morning by morning, wakens my ear to listen like one being taught. The Sovereign LORD has opened my ears, and I have not been rebellious" (Isaiah 50:4–5). God hears our prayers. It may feel as though they are bouncing off the ceiling, and that he is millions of miles away, but he hears. When our daughter Brooke was a little girl, she suffered with eczema. Eczema is a condition that causes very itchy skin. Imagine being two, three, and four years old, and having to refrain from itching. That is an unimaginable task for a child that young. Night after night,

"Give us the first seven years of a child's life, with God's grace, and we may defy the world, the flesh, and the devil to ruin that immortal soul. Those first years, while the clay is yet soft and plastic, go far to decide the form of the vessel. Do not say that your office, you who teach the young, is the least degree inferior to ours, whose main business is with older folks. No, you have the first of them, and your impressions, as they come first, will endure last; oh, that they may be good, and only good!"[8]

year after year, we would tuck her into bed and kneel by her bedside. I can still hear her little voice ask God to take away her itchy skin.

"God, how long will she have to wait?" I would ask. "Please, hear her prayer." The answer didn't come right away, but during this long ordeal, this period of prolonged prayer, we saw God develop her faith muscles. Throughout this entire ordeal, Proverbs 11:28 became my one-sentence prayer over Brooke's condition: "The righteous will thrive like a green leaf." She heard that verse a thousand times, I know, but I was convinced God would fulfill His promise. Not only would she get better, she would thrive.

While on vacation one year, we met a woman who created herbal soaps. "I had a dream one night about a special soap that would help people with eczema and psoriasis," she said.

I cried. My husband smiled—and we bought the soap. Who would have thought an herbal soap would be an answer to prayer? Certainly not us. But, for years, we ordered that herbal soap and saw Brooke's itchy skin slowly disappear. She learned that God answers prayers.

3. Manoah believed God would give the grace to accomplish the task he had been called to complete: the training of Samson.[9]

"Fathers and mothers need to know their children as well as is humanly possible. God knows his children perfectly, knows their thoughts before they think them, knows them through and through. Human fathers and mothers, on the other hand, are not omniscient. They are faced with mystery. Children need help. God gives to fallible parents this little boy or girl, who will certainly prove to be far from perfect, to love and train and teach, to bring up, in the 'nurture and admonition,' the training and instruction, of the Lord. It's a serious assignment. There is no higher calling."[10]

He believed in God's power to enable him to do the job right. Have you heard the expression "What God orders, God pays for"? I can't begin to tell you how many times I have felt inadequate, discouraged, downtrodden, negative, and insecure over the daunting task of raising my three children and managing my home. These feelings always propel me straight to the feet of Jesus, for it is only through his enabling and empowering that I can complete it.

As a preschool creative movement teacher for years, I implemented a tried and true exercise called "mirroring" in all my classes. Children would sit face-to-face and mirror one another's actions. They would follow my example and try to be as exact as possible. They learned to intensely focus on the other individual, accurately interpreting every detail of their facial expressions and movement. Even the tiniest preschooler understood this exercise.

As our eyes focus on Jesus, our every movement should mirror his character. We are the pattern our children are going to mirror. While a sobering thought, it is so true. Will we make mistakes? Will we want to quit? *Absolutely*. But, showered by the grace of God, we will press on and depend daily on God and his Word so we exemplify Christ in all we do. Remember, we only have one chance to raise our children. It is a *now* job.

> "Prayer, like the best conversations on earth, cultivates intimacy, nurtures obedience, and becomes a way of working with God."[11]

4. *Manoah believed that where God gave a child to be trained for His service, He would give the wisdom needed to do so.*[12]

We lack, and God supplies. That's how the economy works in God's kingdom. James 1:5 says, "If any of you lacks wisdom, *he should ask God* [author's italics], who gives generously to all without finding fault, and it will be given to him." Wisdom is highly undervalued in today's society. Watch any sitcom, cartoon, reality television show, commercial, or entertainment show. Within five minutes, some character or celebrity is demonstrating foolish behavior, in stark contrast to wisdom. Ever since my children were little, I have said, "Make wise choices." "Is that wise? Should you do that?" "Should you touch a hot burner on the stove?" "Is it wise to run across the street when a car is coming?"

When situations and circumstances are addressed in this manner, a clear line is drawn. Training them to see the difference between wisdom and folly is imperative. Now, as they prepare to leave the safe haven of home and begin building their own lives, I ask, "Is it wise to get wasted? To abuse alcohol? Is it wise to accrue debt in order to have everything you want? Is it wise to become physically intimate with a girlfriend or boyfriend? Think about the consequences." Proverbs 13:20 serves as our watchword: "He who walks with the wise grows wise, but a companion of fools suffers harm."

What is wisdom? What is folly? Let's compare the two:

Wisdom[13]	Folly[14]
Wisdom is "the right use or exercise of knowledge; the choice of laudable ends, and the best means to accomplish them." Wisdom is strength.	Folly is "weakness of intellect; imbecility of mind; want of understanding." Folly is weakness.
Psalm 111:10 "The fear of the LORD is the beginning of wisdom; all who follow his precepts have good understanding." Key: Follow his precepts.	Proverbs 1:7 "The fear of the LORD is the beginning of knowledge, but fools despise wisdom and discipline." Key: Fools despise his precepts.
Proverbs 9:12 "If you are wise, your wisdom will reward you; if you are a mocker, you alone will suffer." Key: Wisdom yields rewards.	Proverbs 14:24 "The wealth of the wise is their crown, but the folly of fools yields folly. Key: Folly yields folly— consequences.

Look at two key words associated with wisdom: *exercise* and *choice*. Wisdom is active and involves making choices based on knowledge. Manoah asked God to show him the rule and work of his son's life. Then, upon receiving the knowledge concerning the "how to's" of exercising this knowledge, Manoah made choices. Good choices. Choices that would lead to a praiseworthy, impressive, and admirable end. Manoah knew that "the world becomes a strange, mad, painful place and life in it a disappointing and unpleasant business for those who do not know about God. Disregard the study of God, and you sentence yourself to stumble and blunder through life, blindfolded, as it were, with no sense of direction, and no understanding of what surrounds you. This way you can waste your life, and lose your soul."[15]

> Wisdom enlightens and yields rewards. Folly blindfolds and yields severe consequences.

One of the most critical aspects of transforming your home into fortresses of faith is training your children to walk in wisdom and refute folly—from an early age. "Blessed is the man who finds wisdom," writes Solomon, "the man who gains understanding, for she [wisdom] is more profitable than silver and yields better return than gold (Proverbs 3:13–14)." What a tremendous promise. Wisdom enlightens and yields rewards. Folly blindfolds and yields severe consequences . It is as simple as that.

5. He simply prayed.[16]

Don't you love the way Andrew Murray states this—"simply prayed"? Can it be so simple? Yes, it can. Things get so complicated these days and for that reason, parents need simply to pray. There are so many voices. So many experts. So many advertisers vying for our attention. So many schools claiming their academics are the best. So many athletic programs clamoring that they can make our child a shining star. Get them a scholarship. Raising children shouldn't be so complicated. Finding time to be a family shouldn't be so difficult. Perhaps that is why we chose home education for so many years. Somehow, we regained control of our time.

At the onset of parenting, my husband and I had strong convictions as to how we wanted to raise our children. How? One Scripture passage at a time. From Manoah, I learned the profound truth of simply praying. I learned praying doesn't have to be complicated.

6. In conclusion, Manoah saw prayer as three things:[17]

1. The solution to difficulties
2. The supply of need
3. The source of wisdom

Manoah refused to let his inadequacies trap him in a spiral of negative emotions. Neither did he allow a sense of obligation and responsibility to force him to take matters into his own hands, unlike those who tend to rely on their own merits, education, personality, or natural abilities. With a solid confidence in the power of prayer, Manoah proceeded to raise Samson, releasing him into the hands of a powerful God.

> "Groanings which cannot be uttered are often prayers which cannot be refused."[18]

Many others followed Manoah's pattern throughout history. Every morning at 8:30 a.m., Casper Ten Boom, father of Corrie and Betsie ten Boom, read from the "big, brass-hinged Bible"[19] after breakfast. This act of faithfulness proved to be the foundation stone that enabled Betsie and Corrie to endure the unimaginable hardships of Nazi concentration camps.

John Piper writes of Augustine of Hippo, "His mother's praying became the school where he learned deep things about Jesus' words in John 16:24: 'Until now you have not asked for anything in my name. Ask and you will receive, and your joy will be complete.'" Augustine said his mother, Monica, "shed more tears over my spiritual death, than other mothers shed for the bodily death of a son." Years later, Augustine was converted and the rest is history."[20]

Rev. Clarence and Hannah Chambers, parents of Oswald, were challenged by D. L. Moody and Ira Sankey in 1874 (the year of Oswald's birth), and their lives changed. Hannah had "four children in school and four younger ones at home. Her budget was meager and money was scarce, but none suspected that anything less than the abundance of the Almighty was theirs. She greeted each day with joy and each crisis with the assurance that the Lord would provide. Oswald would learn the vital importance of prayer. But because of his earnest faith in God, his prayers seemed to go beyond mere form. His brother Franklin described Oswald's prayers at the age of five as 'very original' and recalled times when the older children, along with their mother, would tiptoe up the stairs at night and sit quietly to hear him pray as he knelt by his bed."[21]

Charles Haddon Spurgeon, sent to live with his grandparents at the age of one, would sit in his grandmother's lap while she read the Bible and prayed and listen to his grandfather's preaching.

Hudson Taylor listened to missionaries tell their grand stories of life on the mission field around the dinner table in his home. Their vision was infectious and marked eight-year-old Hudson's heart with a passion for the lost.

Katherine Gillingham, mother of missionary Elisabeth Elliot, "did not think of herself as deeply spiritual. She would have protested if anyone had said she was. But she was certainly hungry for God, deeply conscious of her own weakness and need for Him. Called to be a mother, entrusted with the holy task of cooperating with God in shaping the destinies of six people, she knew it was too heavy a burden to carry alone. She did not try. She went to Him whose name is Wonderful Counselor, Mighty God, Everlasting Father, and she asked His help."[22]

We, too, are "entrusted with the holy task of cooperating with God"[23] concerning the shaping of our children's destinies. This is a heavy burden to carry alone. Therefore, let us remember not to try. We need to come to the feet of Jesus, who will hear our prayer. In his time, in his way, in his wisdom, he will answer. In closing, hold dear the words of Edwin Keith: "Prayer is exhaling the spirit of man and inhaling the spirit of God."[24]

Time in the Tower

"He Simply Prayed"

1. Prayer is an intangible, something we can't grasp with our hands. Have you struggled with the feeling that prayer is futile? Talk to God about this today. Ask him to help you grasp the power of prayer.

2. Consider simple ways to teach your children the power of prayer. One way is to "sow prayer sensitivity"[25] by reacting to normal everyday occurrences with prayer. Do you hear an ambulance? Pray for the emergency technicians who are helping the patient. Pray for the patient. Do you have any more creative ways to sow prayer sensitivity? Access the article titled "Pray for the Children."[26] Read this stimulating article. Write down five ways you can sow prayer sensitivity.

3. Spend just a moment or two praying a simple one-sentence prayer for your spouse and each of your children. Sentence prayers are the best way for very young children to learn the discipline of prayer. In fact, I am wholeheartedly convinced that sometimes sentence prayers are the most profound. For example:

   "Lord, help Tommy learn to share his toys."

   "God, Suzanne needs to obey my voice on the first command."

   "Lord, be the doctor's hands as he performs Isabella's surgery tomorrow."

   "Wrap your love around Candace today—like a warm blanket on a winter day."

Notes

1. Elisabeth Elliot, South American Mission, http://www.samlink.org/about/prayer.htm.

2. MSN Encarta Dictionary, http://encarta.msn.com/dictionary_/ intangible.html.

3. Ibid.

4. Wayne Grudem, *Systematic Theology* (Leicester, UK, and Grand Rapids, MI: InterVarsity and Zondervan, 1994), 376.

5. Andrew Murray, *Raising Your Children for Christ* (New Kensington, PA: Whitaker House, 1997), 100–01.

6. Dr. Bruce D. Perry, MD, PhD, "Bonding and Attachment in Maltreated Children: Consequences of Emotional Neglect in Childhood," *Scholastic*, http://teacher.scholastic.com/professional/bruceperry/ bonding.htm.

7. Andrew Murray, *Raising Your Children for Christ*, 100.

8. Charles Spurgeon, *Come Ye Children: Practical Help Telling Children about Jesus* (Scotland, UK: Christian Focus Publications Ltd., 2003), 110–11.

9. Andrew Murray, *Raising Your Children for Christ*, 100.

10. Elisabeth Elliot, *The Shaping of a Christian Family* (Grand Rapids, MI: Fleming H. Revell, 1992), 120.

11. Eugene Peterson, *A Year with Jesus* (New York: HarperSanFrancisco, 2006), 59.

12. Andrew Murray, *Raising Your Children for Christ*, 100.

13. Noah Webster, *An American Dictionary of the English Language.*

14. Ibid.

15. J. I. Packer, *Knowing God* (Westmont, IL: InterVarsity, 1993), 14–15.

16. Andrew Murray, *Raising Your Children for Christ,* 101.

17. Andrew Murray, *Raising Your Children for Christ,* 101.

18. Charles Spurgeon, *Character Building for Families,* http://www .characterbuildingforfamilies.com/quotes.html.

19. Elizabeth and John Sherrill, *The Hiding Place* (Grand Rapids, MI: Chosen Books, 2006), 23.

20. John Piper, *The Legacy of Sovereign Joy* (Wheaton, IL: Crossway Books, 2000), 64–66.

21. David McCasland, *Oswald Chambers, Abandoned to God* (Grand Rapids, MI: Discovery House, 1993), 26–27.

22. Elisabeth Elliot, *The Shaping of a Christian Family*, 173.

23. Ibid.

24. Edwin Keith, *The Quote Garden*, http://www.quotegarden.com/prayer.html.

25. Cheri Fuller, *When Children Pray* (Sisters, OR: Multnomah, 1998), 70.

26. Janey L. DeMeo, *Focus on the Family*, "Pray for the Children," http://www.focusonthefamily.com/focusmagazine/spiritualheritage/A000000129.cfm.

SPIRITUAL SUCCESS
Two Fathers, Two Daughters

> "If anyone would come after me, he must deny himself and take up his cross daily and follow me. For whoever wants to save his life will lose it, but whoever loses his life for me will save it. What good is it for a man to gain the whole world, and yet lose or forfeit his very self?" (Luke 9:23–25)

One evening while flipping through the channels, I happened to stumble across a stunning musical production performed by the Disney Junior Symphony. The spotlight had shone on a special nine-year-old concert pianist, described by the commentator as a *prodigy*. At the end of the concert, her father came to the foot of the stage bearing a huge presentation bouquet, hugging her neck, and gleaming with parental pride.

The next day my family ventured to the beach. A few minutes after we set up camp, I watched another father hugging the neck of his daughter—only this time he was carrying her to their beach blanket. She was severely handicapped. Fighting back tears, I watched this man serve this young girl tirelessly. I could only imagine the need he must have for God's sustaining power. I quietly prayed, asking the Lord to pour out his sustaining love on this man and his daughter.

Two fathers. Two daughters. Two extremes.

One father gave flowers; one gave himself. Each of these children is a special gift from God (see Psalm 127:3). There are definite differences between them, but the hand of a loving heavenly Father sculpted both.

As I pondered this, I began to wrestle with their differences. *Why is one so gifted? Why is one so handicapped? It just doesn't seem fair, Lord.*

But as I struggled with these tough questions, I sensed the Lord helping me understand that at the end of our lives, each of us will be judged on our life's journey, not our accolades, our prestigious awards and accomplishments, our mighty deeds, our academic diplomas, or the fortunes we amass, but on the integrity of our character—the stewardship of our thoughts and actions. Did my life bring glory to God? Did I love others deeply? Was I sensitive? Did I fulfill my purpose and destiny? Did I face obstacles with courage and tenacity, ever trusting in his ability to sustain my heart and soul? Was I a cheerful giver? Was I honest and upright? Herein is greatness.

The pursuit of true greatness is a lifelong journey. The world has an array of definitions for this word, identifying *greatness* with fame, fortune, prestige, beauty, athletic prowess, status, academic accomplishment, and superiority of talent. Hence, the sudden onrush of reality shows searching for the next pop star, the next Broadway star, the next sole survivor, the next millionaire, the next top chef, the next top model, the next Fortune 500 apprentice, etc. A plethora of men and women seeking fifteen minutes of fame.

In direct opposition to this we read:

"Whoever wants to become great among you must be your servant" (Matthew 20:26).

"Whoever humbles himself like this child is the greatest in the kingdom of heaven" (Matthew 18:4).

"If anyone wants to be first, he must be the very last, and the servant of all" (Mark 9:35).

Two extremes. One serves self. One serves God.

There is an obvious tension between these two distinctly different perspectives—begging answers to the following questions:

- What does it mean to be great or successful in God's eyes?
- What is spiritual success?
- What character qualities distinguish a great person?
- How do we, as parents, instill God's perspective of spiritual success in our children?

Two specific words emerged as I thought about men and women who are considered spiritually successful: magnanimity and humility. Think about these sterling character qualities.

Magnanimity[1]	*Humility*[2]
Derived from two Latin roots, *magnus*, great, and *animus*, mind.	Derived from Latin *humilius*; supposed to be from humus, the earth.
"Greatness of mind; that elevation or dignity of soul, which encounters danger and trouble with tranquility and firmness, which raises the possessor above revenge, and makes him delight in acts of benevolence, which makes him disdain injustice and meanness, and prompts him to sacrifice personal ease, interest and safety for the accomplishment of useful and noble objects."	"In ethics, freedom from pride or arrogance. In theology, lowliness of mind; a deep sense of one's own unworthiness in the sight of God, self-abasement, penitence for sin, and submission to the divine will."

Magnanimity and humility are two marks of greatness that epitomized Joshua, a great man who lived centuries before the coming of Christ. Meet a young man with astounding attributes whose résumé included:

> "If I have seen further than others it is by standing upon the shoulders of giants."[3]

- Moses' aide since youth (Numbers 11:28)
- The servant of the Lord (Joshua 24:29)
- Eyewitness of the ten plagues, the first Passover, the Red Sea crossing, and the miracles that took place during the forty-year wandering in the wilderness (Exodus 7–17)
- Gallant military leader in the battle against the Amalekites (Exodus 17:8–16)
- Sole companion for Moses on Mount Sinai when God gave Israel the Ten Commandments (Exodus 24:12–18)
- Ardent worshipper and follower of God (Exodus 33:11)
- "A man in whom is the spirit" (Numbers 27:18)
- One of the twelve spies sent to explore the land of Canaan (Numbers 13)
- Brave scout who, alongside his comrade Caleb, courageously denounced the unbelief of the other ten spies—exhorting the Israelites to have faith in God (Numbers 14)
- Successor to Moses as leader of the Israelites (Joshua 1:1–9)

Quite an impressive list of positions, wouldn't you agree? Joshua didn't waste his youth. He stood beside one of the greatest men of all time—Moses. Now, with Moses gone, Joshua was to be his successor.

Pretty big shoes to fill, but Joshua was prepared. Remember, he "did not leave the tent" (Exodus 33:11) but sat in God's presence. I can't help but wonder what happened in that tent of meeting. Oh, to be a fly on the wall.

At the inauguration as the Israelite leader, recorded in Joshua 1, he received explicit instructions on how to be successful. If Joshua 1 were published today, it might be titled, "Joshua's Seven Secrets to Spiritual Success." A certain bestseller—after all, Joshua *was* Moses' right-hand man. Thousands would flock to his success seminars. I know I would. What would Joshua say to his audience? What message would we hear if we sat in on one of his presentations?

More than likely, Joshua's PowerPoint presentation would be taken from Joshua 1:6–9. But before you read it, I want to ask you to do one thing—keep *your* idea of success in the forefront of your mind. As you read, make mental notes comparing Joshua's success principles with your own.

> Be strong and courageous, because you will lead these people to inherit the land I swore to their forefathers to give them. Be strong and very courageous. Be careful to obey all the law my servant Moses gave you; do not turn from it to the right or to the left, that you may be successful wherever you go. Do not let this Book of the Law depart from your mouth; meditate on it day and night, so that you may be careful to do everything written in it. Then you will be prosperous and successful. Have I not commanded you? Be strong and courageous. Do not be terrified; do not be discouraged, for the Lord your God will be with you wherever you go. (Joshua 1:6–9)

Here are "Joshua's Seven Secrets to Spiritual Success."

Spiritual Success Secret #1:
Be strong and very courageous.

Notice the placement of the adverb *very*. Be *very* courageous. It is strategically placed to emphasize the importance of courage. Try replacing *very* with synonyms:

Be *extremely* courageous.
Be *incredibly* courageous.
Be *exceptionally* courageous.
Be *exceedingly* courageous.
Be *extraordinarily* courageous.

Wow! That adds an incredible dimension to the importance of Joshua's first secret. On the threshold of his personal ministry, little did Joshua know what lay ahead of him. Could he have imagined

- crossing the Jordan River on dry ground? (Joshua 3)
- establishing at Gilgal the "Twelve Stones of Remembrance," which would serve as a spiritual tool for parents to teach their children about the faith? (Joshua 4)
- ushering the Israelites into the Promised Land—the fulfillment of God's promise to his predecessor, Moses? (Joshua 5)
- leading massive military campaigns against all the enemy occupants in the new land? (Joshua 6)
- dealing with the sin in the Israelite camps? (Joshua 7)
- seeing the sun stand still? (Joshua 10:13–14)
- conquering six nations and thirty-one kings? (Joshua 11:18–23; 12:24)
- conquering central, southern, and northern Canaan? (Joshua 10–13)
- overseeing the distribution of the land of Canaan to the entire Israelite community? (Joshua 14–19)
- developing the Cities of Refuge? (Joshua 20)
- enjoying rest in the Promised Land? (Joshua 23)

Certainly, at the onset of this new phase of his life, Joshua needed a fresh dose—a renewed impetus—of strength and courage. The giants of the Valley of Eschol were a mere hint of

"Because they have not followed me wholeheartedly, not one of the men twenty years old or more who came up out of Egypt will see the land I promised on oath to Abraham, Isaac and Jacob—not one except Caleb son of Jephunneh the Kenizzite and Joshua son of Nun, for they followed the Lord wholeheartedly." (Numbers 32:11–12)

what was to come in Joshua's life (Numbers 13–14). Even though he evidenced immense courage in his youth, God was bringing him into a period of ministry where even greater courage would be required. I ask myself, *How did a young man face an angry crowd of disagreeable elders who wanted to stone him* (see Numbers 14:10)? *How did a young man bear this type of resistance and rage?*

Somewhere in Joshua's youth, somewhere in his initial training, he received an infusion of courage and humility. Did he catch Moses' spirit? We don't know. We aren't given any information about Joshua's early years. We never meet his parents. We only know he was from the tribe of Ephraim. And, within this tribe, he showed potential for greatness. With limited information, all I can conclude is that Joshua could stand alone in the crowd, risking his life, because he knew the one true God.

We have no idea what our children will be called to face in their lifetime, but, as we introduce them to God and his Word, we are laying the firm foundation of faith and fortitude that will enable them to face anything with strength and courage. Second Corinthians 4:7 says it all: "But we have this treasure in jars of clay to show that this all-surpassing power is from God and not from us." Joshua knew he was a jar of clay, a man who needed the all-surpassing power of God to accomplish anything.

Spiritual Success Secret #2:
Obey the law.

Three words. Simple and direct. Having served beside Moses for most of his life, Joshua was well aware of the law and understood its reciprocity. He understood, firsthand, the severity of disobedience. Shortly after his inauguration, Joshua was faced with the conquest of Ai (Joshua 7). After hearing the report of his spies, "Send two or three thousand men to take it and do not weary all the people, for only a few men are there," instead of depending on God, Joshua sent forth a weak army that was easily defeated. Full of consternation, "Joshua tore his clothes and fell facedown to the ground before the ark of the LORD, remaining there till evening." Not expecting defeat, Joshua fled to the presence of God, knowing something had to be wrong. Here, before God, Joshua received a word from God: "Stand up! What are you doing on your face? Israel has sinned; they have violated my

> *Ai* means "heap of ruins."[4]

covenant, which I commanded them to keep. They have taken some of the devoted things; they have stolen, they have lied, they have put them with their own possessions. That is why the Israelites cannot stand against their enemies; they turn their backs and run because they have been made liable to destruction. I will not be with you anymore unless you destroy whatever among you is devoted to destruction" (Joshua 7:10–13).

Israel was a heap of ruins. There was sin in the camp. Joshua arose from his time with God and settled the situation, finding Achan, from the tribe of Judah, guilty of stealing plunder from Jericho (see Joshua 6:18–19). After summoning Achan, his family, his sheep, his cattle, and his donkeys, along with the stolen goods, Israel stoned them to death in the Valley of Achor—the "Valley of Trouble."

When we don't obey God's laws, the result is a heap of ruins. Achan's disobedience brought destruction on him and his family. May Achan's mistake teach us a valuable lesson: Obey God's laws.

Joshua and Israel moved forward after removing the sin from their camp. They successfully defeated Ai, burned it to the ground (making it a heap of ruins), and hung the king on a tree.

If you find yourself amid a heap of ruins—fall facedown before God and repent. Do whatever it takes to remove the sin from your camp. In doing so, your family will be blessed and God will be glorified.

Spiritual Success Secret #3:
Do not swerve from this law.

Joshua couldn't help but remember that his mentor, Moses, didn't follow God's command completely. Numbers 20 records that God told Moses to "speak to the rock" and it would pour out water, but instead Moses "struck the rock" twice—like he had done before (see Exodus 17:1–7). This one action kept Moses out of the Promised Land. A bit harsh? Perhaps, in our perspective, but obviously God deemed it a lesson for all generations to come. God demands complete obedience and then showers us with the grace to follow him wholeheartedly. He knew Joshua. Remember how Joshua wouldn't leave the tent (Exodus 33:11)? His ardent passion for God would keep him from swerving.

Spiritual Success Secret #4:
Meditate day and night.

Thomas Manton (1620–1677), Puritan preacher and author, might have encouraged Joshua by telling him, "To hear and not to meditate is unfruitful. We hear and hear, but it is like putting a thing into a bag with holes . . . It is rashness to pray and not to meditate. What we take in by the Word we digest by meditation and let out by prayer."[5]

Manton is saying that the Word of God must be ever in the forefront of our minds; guiding our decisions and actions minute by minute, night and day. Not strict, rigid laws, but grace-filled guidelines and directives that promise provision and success for every detail of our lives. Isn't it encouraging that even a man like Joshua—valiant and forthright—had to be instructed to meditate (Joshua 1:7)? Somehow, I find that comforting.

Spiritual Success Secret #5:
Do not be terrified.

Pretty self-explanatory, don't you agree? Joshua knew whom he would be up against—Canaanites, Hittites, Hivites, Perizzites, Girgashites, Amorites, and Jebusites. All big, strong, mighty enemies of God. God, who sits on the throne of heaven, is offering reassurance and infusing confidence into the spirit of Joshua—who we know has already proved his valor many, many times.

As a parent, I have faced terrifying situations. Long nights in the emergency room, waiting to see if the Tylenol my toddler son ingested was at toxic levels. Years of terrifying thoughts concerning my daughter's bouts with alopecia areata—would she go bald? And so many more. In the face of adversity, a courageous spirit develops and matures. In the face of terrifying situations, dependence on God becomes the anchor of our hope (see Hebrews 6:19).

Spiritual Success Secret #6:
Do not be discouraged.

Ahhh, discouragement. The devil's greatest tool. Discouragement is nothing more than the "depression of confidence or hope; the act of depriving of courage."[6] Here's where I want to dissect the definition of magnanimity. Stop and listen. A magnanimous person

- encounters danger and trouble with tranquility and firmness;
- delights in acts of benevolence;
- sacrifices personal ease, interest, and safety for the accomplishment of useful and noble objects.[7]

Let these attributes sink into your soul. When my children were very young, I came across a prayer penned by missionary Amy Carmichael. Written by a woman who never married, but mothered hundreds of little children in India, her keen insight into a child's need for magnanimity and humility astounded me. I took notice of her wisdom and began praying the prayer over my children. Her pen served as a sword as it cut to the quick of raising a godly child.

The Parent's Prayer

Make _____ (insert names) good soldiers of Jesus Christ;
    let them never turn back in the day of battle.
Let them be winners and helpers of souls.
Let them live not to be ministered to, but to minister.
Make them loyal; let them set loyalty high above all things.
Make them doers, not mere talkers.
Let them enjoy hard work and choose hard things rather than easy.
Make them trustworthy. Make them wise, for it is written,
    "He hath no pleasure in fools."
Let them pass from dependence on us to dependence on Thee.
Let them never come under the dominion of earthly things; keep
    them free.
Let them grow up healthy, happy, friendly, and keen to make others happy.

Give them eyes to see the beauty of the world and hearts to wor-
    ship its Creator.
Let them be gentle to beast and bird; let cruelty be hateful to them.
May they walk, O Lord, in the light of thy countenance.
And for ourselves, we ask that we might never weaken.
"God is my strong salvation."
We ask that we might train them to say that word and live that life,
    and pour themselves out for others unhindered by self. Amen.

Spiritual Success Secret #7:
Order your life and family.

Joshua begins putting the secrets to work. He orders the officers
to rally the tribes and ready the supplies. It is time to move.
Time to possess the long-awaited Promised Land (see Joshua
1:10–11). Order precedes any great movement of God. God
orders, man moves. Joshua was a man of understanding and
knowledge; therefore, he maintained order (see Proverbs 28:2).

As I exit Joshua's seminar, I have to ask, "Are these the pri-
orities we put before our children? How are we handling the
tension between the world's view of success and God's view of
success? This tension plays out on a soccer field, basketball
court, theatrical stage, college application, school selection,
classroom, science lab, SAT score, report card, etc.

As a parent, I have to know where I stand on this issue.
Why? Because I will inherently pass this view on to my children.
They will know my perspective; my body language, facial
expressions, and off-the-cuff comments will relay it to them
loud and clear. Having grown up in the world of competitive
dance and beauty pageants, I am completely aware of the allure
of worldly success. I wanted to be famous—or so I thought.
But, at what cost? The fury of the competitive world, with its
comparisons and criticisms, was burning up my sensitive soul.

"A tap dancer's thighs don't jiggle, Janell," said Miss Mary Martin, a local theatre director who was coaching and critiquing the talent portion of my upcoming Miss Virginia Pageant performance. "You must do something about that."

I guess running four to five miles a day and starving myself to death isn't good enough. I'll step it up, I thought.

"And that evening gown looks like it was made out of upholstery fabric. Get rid of that dress," she sneered.

For most of my life, I stood in front of mirrors. That's what dancers do. I listened to other people dictate how I should walk, talk, dance, sit down, stand up, dress, wear my hair, and live my life. Programmed by the opinions of others, I honestly didn't have a clue who I was—on the inside. Not until Jesus Christ came into my life, that is. There, in an ordinary dorm room, God overwhelmed me with his unconditional love and acceptance the dawn of my senior year in college (1980). From that moment, I entered into a personal relationship with him, experiencing a radical life change. My life had been one fraught with angst, anxiety, and apprehension, but after my conversion, I became enveloped in a serious search for knowing my true identity in Christ. The emptiness had been constricting any sense of happiness or purpose. Somewhere deep in my soul I knew there had to be more in life than false praise, flattery, and pleasing man.

Twenty-seven years later, my oldest daughter entered the same search. Even though raised in a fortress of faith, the tension and pull of the world still exists for her. Obviously not to the same degree as for nonbelievers, but it exists. Fully confident in God, she still feels the lure of worldly success and the trap of pleasing man. I asked her if she would be willing to put her struggles down on paper. Now, on the dawn of her last year of college, she shares her heart. She was hesitant at first, but I encouraged her to be "strong and very courageous":

Success. The very word makes me cringe. What is it? More-over, how do you define it? In the ever-daunting college search my last two years of high school, I found myself consumed with others' impressions of my future plans and success, the kind of success parents love to brag about: high test scores, an astronomical GPA, acceptance letters from prestigious uni-versities, exhausting extracurricular involvement, athletic achievements . . . the list goes on. Yet, at the same time, I was rebelling against the other extreme—the mega-Christian idea of success: plans to attend a well-known Christian college, go into missions or the ministry, which can be—at times—a nar-row and inflexible perspective of success. So here I am, torn, unsure, and depressed. What if I'm not really happy with either perspective of success? Well, I wasn't, not for the last two years of high school and the first two of college. Aspira-tions to an Ivy League school, a prestigious undergraduate business school, and a high-powered, big-income job came to signify my idea of success, without my even realizing it. I was enthralled with "the wow factor": the "Good for you!" I received from people every time I said I had applied to Har-vard. And then, when I mentioned I was majoring in finance and planning on applying to the highly esteemed Commerce School at The University of Virginia, where I attend, I loved the reaction it engendered—people were impressed, remark-ing, "Oh, your parents must be so proud" and "You're doing so well."

Well, what if underneath it all . . . I wasn't? What if I felt empty? Which it just so happened I did. I was so distraught I left a résumé workshop in tears.

"You need more extracurricular activities, dear. Possibly be active in more organizations on campus," the counselor said.

"Isn't it enough that I maintain a 3.9–4.0 GPA, work fifteen to twenty hours a week, play in a worship band with Campus Crusade for Christ, and continue honing my songwriting/singing talents? Is more always better? When is enough, enough?" I cried.

Drowning in despair, I was confused—how was this happening? How were my career aspirations so secure yet my hope so insecure? The Bible says, "We have this hope as an anchor for the soul" (Hebrews 6:19). Anchor? That image implies a lot more security in God's plan than I had ever felt up to that point. I wasn't happy with the way the world defined success, yet I didn't see myself fitting the stereotypical mold of Christian success either. Then it hit me. I could be successful in God's eyes even if the whole world, both secular and Christian spheres, thought I was crazy.

What would happen if I stopped looking to others to define success for me and looked only to what God wants for me? For me that meant sacrificing the security of a business degree to be an English major—something I knew would give me more happiness and fulfillment. And even now, nine times out of ten, when remarking I'm an English major, I'm asked, "Oh, you want to be a teacher?" Once more, the world attempts to put me in some box, to define me in some paradigm, but I refuse.

"No, actually," I reply, "I want to be a songwriter."

I've learned that it's okay to live day by day, seeking what God wants for my life, learning what it means to have His hope as an anchor for my soul, an anchor for my future."

"You, dear children, are from God and have overcome them, because the one who is in you is greater than the one who is in the world. They are from the world and therefore speak from the viewpoint of the world, and the world listens to them. We are from God, and whoever knows God listens to us." (1 John 4:4–6)

The transformation in my daughter's heart has been amazing to watch. Painful, yes, but amazing. Can you sense the tension and angst neatly tucked in between the lines? Her college experience has been difficult, to say the least, primarily because God has broken her need to succeed. This isn't the college experience I would have designed for my daughter, but obviously God had other ideas. He wanted her whole heart—a heart like Caleb's and Joshua's—completely yielded to his plan and purpose for her life. Once driven by ego and pride, she now walks in humility and dependence on God. Once striving to make her mark in the world, she now knows that the only place she needs to be is in the center of God's will.

Here it is. This is the bottom line. How do we live a spiritually successful life in this world without being of this world?

A great debate over this subject matter exploded in my living room last night. My son, Grant, was selected to be second seed on his varsity tennis team—which surprised all of us. I hadn't thought much about it—until he mentioned, "Mom, I didn't even play a singles match last year, I was seventh seed, and now I am second seed. I have to play the second seed of all these really good teams."

His dad tried to encourage him. "Son, just pretend you are playing me. It's the same thing."

"Dad, it's not the same thing. Come on, really. This is a competition. If I lose, I let the team down. If I lose, it will be in the paper tomorrow."

The debate between father and son continued, laden with much frustration. After a few minutes, it subsided and everyone went to bed, except me. I waited, then went in to say goodnight to Grant. Our nightly ritual.

"Grant, I want to encourage you to read the first chapter of Joshua before tomorrow's match," I said. "It's really great and I think it might help."

"Mom, why are you and Dad making such a big deal about this?" he said, obviously still frustrated. So I let him talk.

"Mom, playing a match is different than playing Dad. Why can't he understand that?"

"Grant, he does. Trust me, Dad understands competition. But, he's tired and just trying to help. Give him some credit."

"But when people look in the paper the day after my match, it isn't going to say, 'Grant Rardon played his best. He honored God.' It is going to say I won or lost. Period. People are going to walk up to me and ask me, 'Did you win?' They are not going to ask me, 'Did you play with all your heart? Did you do the best you could?' No, they are going to ask me if I won or lost. Period."

"You're right," I responded. "That is exactly what people do. But God looks in your heart. He sees that you have given your all. And that, my son, is what you will be held accountable for. Period. You have to come to the place where the opinions of others don't matter anymore. It doesn't matter what the paper says. What matters is that you have been faithful with your gift, practiced as hard as you could, given it your all, and played with your whole heart. If you win, fantastic! I love it when you win. I love it when you receive rewards. But, what I love *most* is seeing you give it 100 percent effort and heart. And I can't help but think that is what God loves most, as well."

Grant was feeling the tension. The next day, he won his doubles match, but lost in singles. But, he played well. He played with heart. He gave it his best shot—literally. His opponent's mother commented, "Wow, he's gonna be great, in a short amount of time."

With a big smile on my face, I couldn't help but agree. "Yes, he will be great—in time." Little did she know the big debate in which our family had just been engaged.

Jesus resolves the tension of this debate in his last recorded prayer on earth:

I will remain in the world no longer, but they are still in the world, and I am coming to you. Holy Father, protect them by the power of your name—the name you gave me—so that they may be one as we are one. While I was with them, I protected them and kept them safe by that name you gave me. None has been lost except the one doomed to destruction so that Scripture would be fulfilled. I am coming to you now, but I say these things while I am still in the world, so that they may have the full measure of my joy within them. I have given them your word and the world has hated them, for they are not of the world any more than I am of the world. My prayer is not that you take them out of the world but that you protect them from the evil one. They are not of the world, even as I am not of it. Sanctify them by the truth; your word is truth. As you sent me into the world, I have sent them into the world. For them I sanctify myself, that they too may be truly sanctified. (John 17:11–19)

Jesus is very clear: "My prayer is not that you take them out of the world but that you protect them from the evil one." He clarifies that you and I are not of this world. *In* it, but not *of* it. And in order to live successfully, we have been given the Truth. Pastor John Hanneman, in his sermon titled "The Humility of God," explains.

To be humble means that no matter our position, status, title or degree, we are willing to lay aside these things to serve other people in a very earthy, lowly sort of way. It doesn't mean that we can't have status or positions of honor; it means that serving others is never beneath us. His act of stooping to wash another's feet, to humbly serve them, reverses the order of the world's ideas of greatness, rank and significance. It turns the world upside down, because its authority comes from position, title, power and control. Can you imagine

Donald Trump getting on his hands and knees and washing the apprentice's feet, instead of saying, "You're fired"? Can you imagine Bill Gates making coffee for the secretaries? Can you imagine the disgruntled receiver Terrell Owens helping to pass out towels to the other players? Or how about Tiger Woods cleaning the clubs of tour rookies? This isn't how the world operates, but it is how God operates.[8]

Some of the proudest moments of my parenting have been those when I see my children serving others—placing the needs of someone else above their own. As a sophomore in high school, Candace, a novice basketball player, was a bench warmer on her school's varsity basketball team. Though faithful at every practice and eager to learn, she got only a minute or two of playing time each game. But, true to her character, she took care of the five starting players, offering them water and towels on time-outs, cleaning up after games, and cheering them on wholeheartedly. Her father and I considered that season a great success—in every way. She learned spiritual life lessons that will yield benefits the rest of her life.

As long as we live on this planet, in this world we call home, we will feel the inevitable tension between worldly success and spiritual success:

| Worldly Success | | Spiritual Success |

And John offers the perfect balancing bar in 1 John 2:15–17: "Do not love the world or anything in the world. If anyone loves the world, the love of the Father is not in him. For everything in the world—the cravings of sinful man, the lust of his eyes and the boasting of what he has and does—comes not from the Father but from the world. The world and its desires pass away, but the man who does the will of God lives forever."

Not even a Fortune 500 company can promise my daughter that kind of security. And no newspaper can record my son's search for spiritual success—but God knows. Somewhere in the midst of John 17 and 1 John 2:15–17 the tension between worldly success and spiritual success eases. The blurry line separating the two becomes clearer. Can you see that? Isn't it freeing?

After our arduous debate, I think we can safely conclude that spiritual success can joyfully be described as teaching "us to say 'No' to ungodliness and worldly passions, and to live self-controlled, upright and godly lives in this present age, while we wait for the blessed hope—the glorious appearing of our great God and Savior, Jesus Christ" (Titus 2:12–13). It won't be easy—Satan will make sure of that—but God's enabling grace will help us resist the lure.

Remember that beauty pageant I was training so hard for? During the evening gown phase of that competition, I remarked, in front of hundreds of people and a television viewing audience, "Work for the Lord. The work is hard, the hours are long, and the pay is low, but the retirement benefits are out of this world!"[9] Some of my Christian friends told me that was a big mistake. Imagine that.

"That comment is going to hurt you, Janell. They don't like preaching," they laughed. "They are going to laugh you off the stage."

"Hmm," I thought for a moment. "Maybe so, but I'd rather please God than worry about what they are going to think. Who knows—maybe someone will hear it and think about God."

Call me naïve or zealous, but I have never regretted that decision. I didn't win the title of Miss Virginia that fateful night, but twelve months later was crowned "Mrs. Robert V. Rardon." God had a better plan for my life. A very successful one.

Time in the Tower

Two Fathers, Two Daughters

How can you train your children to say "no" to ungodliness (as in Titus 2:12–13 above)? Write down three things you can begin doing today—right now. For example:

1. We will turn off the television when something ungodly comes on.
2. We will read a short passage of Scripture before bedtime.
3. We will serve in our community by _____.

Notes

1. Noah Webster, *An American Dictionary of the English Language* (New York: S. Converse, 1828). Facsimile first edition (Chesapeake, VA: Foundation for American Christian Education, 1967 and all subsequent editions).

2. Ibid.

3. Isaac Newton, "The Quotations Page," http://www.quotationspage.com/quote/862.html (accessed January 20, 2007).

4. *New Analytical Bible and Dictionary of the Bible* (Iowa Falls: World Bible Publishers, 1973), 29.

5. Thomas Manton, as quoted in *Spiritual Disciplines for the Christian Life* by Donald S. Whitney (Colorado Springs: NavPress, 1991), 73.

6. Noah Webster, *An American Dictionary of the English Language*.

7. Ibid.

8. John Hanneman, Peninsula Bible Church Cupertino, *The Humility of God*, http://www.pbcc.org/sermons/hanneman/1379.html (accessed February 20, 2007).

9. Church Signs, http://wilk4.com/humor/humorc13.htm.

OBEDIENCE
No Mumbling, No Grumbling!

My son and I loved going on little dates when he was young. Going to the mall was always at the top of our list of things to do. There was always something to pick up. Our habit was to park by the entrance of a main satellite store. Outside this one particular store's entrance was a dirt pathway about four feet long.

> "Obedience is the fruit of faith;
> Patience the bloom on the fruit." (Author unknown)

One day I mentioned to Grant, "Oh, look, a pathway, just for us! Let's travel through the path together. Let's pretend it is a bridge over a moat and that a castle is on the other side!" Well, he loved the idea, as any imaginative, adventurous little boy would.

Little did I know that from that point on, every time we went to the mall, we had to enter by traveling down the narrow pathway. For years, he referred to it as "our path." Now a mature young man, he denies it, of course. Every trip down the path brought Matthew 7:14 to life: "But small is the gate and narrow the road that leads to life, and only a few find it." Then and there, I would silently pray, "Lord, keep Grant on the narrow path that leads to life. May he be one of the few."

Recorded in Genesis 22 is the amazing account of another young boy's adventure with a pathway. This pathway didn't lead to a mall, but is part of a timeless tale about wholehearted obedience and sacrifice. Young Isaac, the child of promise, traveled three days with his father, Abraham, to the region of Moriah to make a sacrifice to God. Undoubtedly, Isaac had participated in building altars countless times with his father, but this time was to be different. *Isaac was to be the offering.*

Climbing the mountain God had directed them to, Isaac asked a simple question: "Father, the fire and the wood are here, but where is the lamb for the burnt offering?"

With his heart in his throat, Abraham must have cried out to God, "How do I explain this to him? What do I say? Give me the words, Lord."

Isaac illustrated for generations to come a beautiful picture of submission. It truly baffles my mind how a young boy, probably under the age of twelve, would

> "Isaac caught his father's spirit."[1]

crawl up on an altar, knowingly, and lie down. Can you imagine? We see no evidence that Isaac resists, runs, or rebels. He doesn't even complain. He simply asks a practical question concerning the supplies for the sacrifice.

Isaac's obedience is the fruit of Abraham's faith. By lying prostrate upon the altar, Isaac's very position demonstrates to us humility and complete resignation to his father's commands. F. B. Meyer writes concerning Isaac,

> He caught his father's spirit. We do not know how old he
> was; he was at least old enough to sustain the toil of a long
> march on foot and strong enough to carry up the hill the

wood, laid upon his shoulders by his father. Inspiration draws a veil over that last tender scene—the father's announcement of the mission; the broken sobs; the kisses, wet with tears; the instant submission of the son, who was old enough and strong enough to rebel if he had a mind. Then the binding of that tender frame; which, indeed, needed no compulsion, because the young heart had learned the secret of obedience and resignation.[2]

How had Isaac learned this secret of obedience? Genesis 22 gives us insight into the fruit of his obedience, but no real, tangible insight into the how-to's of Abraham's parenting skills. Up to this point, we hear very little about Abraham and Isaac's relationship, but we know they had at least ten to twelve years together prior to Moriah. Considering that Abraham was called God's friend (see Isaiah 41:8, 2 Chronicles 20:7, and James 2:23), Abraham and God had a viable relationship—full of communication and experiences. Day after day, Isaac watched his father, Abraham, live a faith-filled life. Not a perfect life, but one that exemplified a complete trust in God. These observations impacted Isaac's spiritual growth. "The more we come to know a person," writes Wayne Grudem, "and the more we see in that person a pattern of life that warrants trust, the more we find ourselves able to place trust in that person to do what he or she promises, or to act in ways that we can rely on."[3]

"When people have true information about Christ, they are better able to put their trust in him. Moreover, the more we know about him, the more fully we are able to put our trust in him. Thus faith is not weakened by knowledge but should increase with more true knowledge."[4]

The relationship between Abraham and Isaac exemplifies three significant truths that we, as parents, can model for our children:

1. Abraham testifies that we are not to withhold anything from God.
When God asks, we must obey—*the first time.* This is wholehearted obedience. God isn't going to count to three—God's children must obey the first time he asks. In a culture where disrespect is preeminent, I must be vigilant to train my children to so obey. I am dumbfounded at the disrespectful behavior that I see—even among Christian young adults. Could it be that the disrespectful examples of professional athletes, pop music stars, and television and movie characters have somehow infiltrated their minds? If so, parents must be even more vigilant.

Theologians wrestle with the "why's" of the Moriah experience. Could it be that God established Abraham's sacrifice of Isaac as a prototype for generations to come? Isaac was a gift from God (see Genesis 21:1–7). Human nature tends to be tight-fisted. We want to hold on to the gifts of God.

Several years ago, I faced a tight-fisted moment. Candace had graduated from high school and was venturing off to college. Many, many women had tried to prepare me for that fateful day when I was to help her move into her dorm room and leave her—alone in the world. Well, nothing they said prepared me for the intense emotion that flooded my heart and soul. Wave upon wave of emotions washed over me—first *fear* flooded in, whispering, "How will she make it without you? You can't leave her here. She is panicked—you can see it all over her."

Then *despair* chimed in, "Oh, what have you done? Why did you let her go away to school?"

Sheer sadness rolled in next: "When will you see her again? Things will never be the same, you know; your little family is forever changed."

Finally, *grief* attempted to drown me once and for all: "It's all over. Say 'good-bye' to the way things were."

I know I cried for three hours straight. My sweet husband, who was seemingly fine with this turning point in our life, gave me space—allowing me ample time to work through the severe separation anxiety. Wise man. It was during this period of letting go that I reminded myself of the letter I had written her the night before and left under her pillow in her dorm room:

Well, dear daughter, eighteen years ago, God gave me the most remarkable gift in you. I can still remember our first hours together—you lying on my chest, sleeping soundly. It was one of the greatest days of my life. Now, today, I have to let you go. Dona Maddux Cooper says it best: "When you were small and just a touch away, I covered you with blankets against the cold night air. But now that you are tall and out of reach, I fold my hands and cover you with prayer." You will not be in my reach anymore—but my prayers will cover you. I thank the Lord that I have been reading Isobel Kuhn's amazing work *Green Leaf in Drought-Time*. God truly ordered my finding this book, for it has prepared me for this difficult passage. Remember how I told you the story of missionaries Arthur, Wilda, and Lilah (their infant girl) Mathews being nearly starved to death in northern China by the Red regime? Never have I read such an incredible story of heroism and courage. Isobel Kuhn's account of their plight is compelling. In October of 1951, the local police had stalled their finances. In the face of starvation, Arthur Mathews wrote, "From the writings of Charles Fox, I read today, "Now shalt thou see what I will do." He continued, "Five smooth stones. There are five stones which will bring down any giant. They are: God is, God has, God can, God will, God does."[5]

Wilda's response was equally poignant. Psalm 91 had been their mantra throughout this entire ordeal—but while reading through it again one day, Psalm 91:4 (KJV) arrested their attention: "He shall cover thee with His feathers, and under His wings shalt thou trust."

"Arthur's poetic mind seized on the imagery," Isobel writes. She described Arthur's reaction to this verse: " 'Wilda! This is the feather curtain of God. The mother-bird's wings come down over the little chicks and they are sheltered from whatever is attacking. Cuddled up close to the mother-hen all they see are her feathers around them—and that is all we are supposed to look at! The feather wings of God sheltering us!' "[6]

So, dear daughter, I leave you resting under the feather curtain of God. I've enclosed a small feather—keep it in front of you as a reminder of how much God loves you and that no matter what difficulties you face this year: "God is, God has, God can, God will, and God does."[7]

More than fifty years ago, amid austere circumstances, Arthur Mathews discovered the secret to finding peace amid overwhelming, life-threatening circumstances. His discovery led me to mine: I needed to trust God.

No, I wasn't being starved to death, but I had to let go of a very big part of my reason for existing here on earth. The basic training and raising of my oldest child was over. Finished. As I moved through the process and quieted myself, I remembered that life had held other challenges for me. With God's strength, I had faced the obstacle of growing up with an alcoholic father. What Satan had intended for evil, God restored. When my pastor and his wife died within a year of each other, God helped me. When I miscarried our second child, God walked me through that pain and two years later gave me twins. When my father fell victim to cancer and died, God met me in his hospital room, restoring years of anguish and hate with a visitation of joy. When my mother-in-law died suddenly of a staph infection, God upheld my husband and me. Slowly, I remembered that every time life became difficult and too much to bear, God was there to see me through.

So there in my hotel room, amid my emotional pain and agony, I whispered, "Okay, Lord, I am going to trust you again. I am not going to withhold my daughter from you. I release her into your care. Help me crawl up under the shadow of your wings and rest. Hide me behind the feather curtain. This is a dark tunnel, but I'm going to look for the light."

The light came. It took months, but finally, God shed his light. While walking through the Art Institute of Chicago, I happened upon an incredible picture entitled, "Winged Figure" by American artist Abbot Henderson Thayer (1889).[8] This magnificent painting opened my spiritual eyes and helped me to envision Psalm 91. In this picture was an angel in total repose. As I fixed my eyes on this painting, I began to conceptualize "resting" and "dwelling" under the shadow of the Almighty. Her hand's poignant position over her breast signifies allegiance, trust, and complete confidence in the Creator of the universe. Herein lies the secret to always having a serene soul and strength of purpose, resting in the knowledge that God is in complete control of every aspect of our lives— *every* aspect.

> "The feather curtain of God falls silently. It is soft and cuddly to the sheltered one; but intangible, mysterious and baffling to the outsider."[9]

From that moment on, I purposed to live my life according to the promises and conditions of Psalm 91. This special psalm speaks of hiddenness, submission, and trust. I wanted to hide in the shadow of the Almighty's wings—especially when life makes no sense. Here, withdrawn from public view, I begin building a friendship with God and learning to dwell in his presence. Donald S. Whitney writes,

The more we focus on God, the more we understand and appreciate how worthy He is. As we understand and appreciate this, we can't help but respond to Him. Just as an incredible sunset or a breathtaking mountaintop vista evokes a spontaneous response, so we cannot encounter the worthiness of God without the response of worship. If you could see God at this moment, you would so utterly understand how worthy He is of worship that you would instinctively fall on your face and worship Him.[10]

Abraham knew God in this way. He knew that the secret to our stability, serenity, and security lies in our ability to stay close to the heart of God. When I consider residing in the shadow of the Almighty, I actually see myself climbing upward and crawling up and under his wings. As well as a shelter, it is an elevated vantage point that helps me see my condition, my problems, and my life from a heavenly point of view. Our heavenly Father, who resides on his throne in heaven, sees the big picture. We only see in part.

Activate this potential by climbing upward into the shadow of God's wings. There, hidden from public view and close to the heart of God, rest. Like Isaac, lie down on the altar of God's faithfulness. Silence the questions. Silence your heart. Listen. Know you're safe and sound under the feather curtain of God.

2. Isaac learned that at every Moriah, God will provide.

Abraham renamed the place where he had built the altar "The Lord Provides" (*Jehovah-jireh*). He had no idea a ram would be waiting in the thicket. Imagine the moment: Abraham, with knife in hand, prepares to thrust the knife into Isaac's heart, when all of a sudden he hears God ordering him, "Do not lay a hand on the boy. Do not do anything to him" (Genesis 22:12). Because Abraham didn't withhold anything, God speaks to him through an angel, saying, "I swear by myself . . . that because you have done this and have not withheld your son, your only son, I will surely bless you and make your descendants as numerous as the stars in the sky and the sand on the seashore."

God always provides. Money to pay the bills. Help for a struggling student. Food for the table. Gas for the car. Creative ideas for saving money. Take a minute and write down all the many ways God has provided for you and your family. It is good to remember the good-ness of God. *Provision* means "preparation; measures taken beforehand, either for security, defense or attack, or for the sup-ply of wants."[11] I love the empha-sis on "measures taken beforehand."[12] Isn't it comforting to know that God, our Provider, has taken measures beforehand to make provision for our families?

> Abraham had absolutely no idea a ram would be waiting in the thicket.

My husband and I didn't know it at the time, but our hon-eymoon was a foreshadowing of our financial future. Hours into our new life together, we had a flat tire and were told we needed four new tires. *Thank you, God, for our wedding money.* Did we want to spend it on tires? *No way!* But God "had taken measures beforehand" to give us exactly what we needed for new tires. On our way home, we stopped and had just enough money for our last lunch. We came home from our honey-moon with one penny. I kid you not. *One penny.* At the time, it seemed cute and quaint, but in reality it was a real-life lesson concerning the provision of God. We have always had enough for what we need—maybe not for what we want—but for what we need.

Somehow, knowing that God "takes measures beforehand" for that which we need offers a sense of security and deep, abid-ing peace. Paul says it best in 1 Timothy 6:17: "Command those who are rich in this present world not to be arrogant nor to put their hope in wealth, which is so uncertain, but to put their hope in God, who richly provides us with everything for our enjoyment."

3. Isaac learned to lie down on altars.

We might call this "submission" in its greatest form. Derived from the Latin root *submitto*—*sub*, or under, and *mitto*, to send—submission simply means "resignation." *Resignation* is "a quiet submission to the will of Providence. Submission without discontent and with entire acquiescence."[13]

Herein lies the truest goal of the rock-solid family— *training your children to submit to and follow God.* Once again, I return to Andrew Murray's wise advice on training our children in obedience.

> Train is a word of deep importance for every teacher and parent to understand. It is not telling, not teaching, not commanding, but something higher than all of these. Without training, teaching and commanding often do more harm than good. Training is not only telling a child what to do, but showing him how to do it and seeing that it is done. The parent must see to it that the advice or the command given is put into practice and adopted as a habit. Success in education depends more on forming habits than instilling rules. What the child has done once or twice he must learn to do over and over again, until it becomes familiar and natural. In this way the habit of obedience is formed and becomes the root of other habits.[14]

The habit of obedience was evident in young Isaac. There is no reason to believe that Isaac mumbled, grumbled, or resisted Abraham. It is not noted that he even complained. How in the world is this possible? In today's world, children mumble and grumble over everything, it seems, unless trained to do otherwise. One of the most critical elements in learning to obey is to "Do everything without complaining or arguing" (Philippians 2:14). And I believe we could add murmuring, mumbling, and grumbling.

Say the word *mumble* ten times. Now multiply that sound by a household of people doing the same. Does it not have a droning undertone that completely annoys? *Grumbling has the same effect.* In the purest sense of the word, grumble means to "murmur with discontent."[15]

- Murmur (v.i.): to make a low, continued noise, like the hum of bees; to utter complaints in a low, half-articulated voice; to utter sullen discontent.[16]
- Discontent (n): uneasiness or inquietude of mind; dissatisfaction at any present state of things.[17]

It is so easy to mumble and grumble. The Israelites did it for forty years. Laden with discontent, they transformed a quick trip into forty years of wandering. Now, as a parent, I do not want wandering children.

As soon as a child can speak, a parent must be diligent to train that child to "do everything without complaining or arguing." Once again, vigilance is required. Day after day, minute by minute, as parents, we must extinguish such behavior with consistent effort.

Abraham's training manifested itself as a sweet, fragrant fruit for years to come. May God enable us to follow in the footsteps of this great patriarch of our faith. May our children, as did Isaac, obey wholeheartedly—honoring their parents with a life well lived.

Time in the Tower

No Mumbling, No Grumbling!

So many of us battle with mumbling, murmuring, and grumbling. Are you ready to wage war on these triplets of disobedience? Here's how:

1. Establish an action plan. First, as man and wife, sit together and decide on your plan of attack. What will the consequences be for such undesirable communication? What will the rewards be for new patterns of communication?
2. Call a family meeting. Obviously, if you have small children (under the age of two), this isn't the plan for you, but as a family make a strong commitment to hold one another accountable.
3. Chart the new, healthy patterns of communication expected, such as:
   - I will be careful not to mumble, murmur, or grumble.
   - I will obey the first time I am asked to do something.
   - I will guard my words and use them wisely.
   - If I am upset about something, I will go to my room and calm down. Then, I will go and calmly talk to the person with whom I am upset.
   - I will be cautious not to disrespect those in authority over me.
   - I will put a penny in the "Mumble No More" jar on the kitchen counter every time I mumble, murmur, or complain. (Perhaps each child can start out with 100 pennies at the beginning of the month. Be creative. Older children can start out with a roll of quarters—out of their own money, of course.)

Notes

1. F. B. Meyer, *Abraham* (Fort Washington, PA: Christian Literature Crusade, 1983), 137.

2. Ibid.,137–38.

3. Wayne Grudem, *Systematic Theology* (Leicester, UK, and Grand Rapids, MI: InterVarsity and Zondervan, 1994), 711.

4. Ibid., 712.

5. Isobel Kuhn, *Green Leaf in Drought-Time* (Chicago: Moody Press, 1957), 65.

6. Ibid., 66.

7. Ibid.

8. Abbot Henderson Thayer, *Winged Figure*. A view of this incredible picture is available online at: http://www.oceansbridge.com/oil-paintings/section.php?xSec=2510.

9. Isobel Kuhn, *Green Leaf in Drought-Time*, 72.

10. Donald S. Whitney, *Spiritual Discipline for the Christian Life* (Colorado Springs: NavPress, 1991), 87.

11. Noah Webster, *An American Dictionary of the English Language* (New York: S. Converse, 1828). Facsimile first edition (Chesapeake, VA: Foundation for American Christian Education, 1967 and all subsequent editions).

12. Ibid.

13. Ibid.

14. Andrew Murray, *Raising Your Children For Christ* (Fort Kensington, PA: Whitaker House, 1997), 133–35.

15. Noah Webster, *An American Dictionary of the English Language*.

16. Ibid.

17. Ibid.

LOVE
Training the Tongue

> "While in our family there were plenty of times of uproarious laughter, times when we were allowed to play hide-and-seek in the house on a rainy day, times when we could not help shouting, running, jumping, and thundering up and down the stairs, we were taught to think first—was someone asleep, was Daddy studying, did Mother have a headache? Quiet was the general rule. Gentle voices, soft footsteps, the quiet closing of doors contribute to the peace of the home. Learning these simple things is learning to look to the interests of others rather than to one's own. If we thoughtlessly slammed a door (it was hard to remember that big screen door in the summertime) we were asked to come back into the house and do it right."[1]

D o you like it when someone calls you a name?" I asked my children's church class. "What does it do to your heart when someone throws a critical name your way?"

The children sat silent, considering the question with great concern. Jason raised his hand. "It hurts bad!"

Cathy commented, "It makes me want to run and cry, just run away!"

Another interjected, "It makes me want to hit 'em!"

All these comments are accurate and honest reflections concerning the enduring game of name-calling. Have you ever noticed you don't have to teach a child to be mean? It seems to come with the territory. So, it is your responsibility to teach them it is wrong to call another person names. Why? Because name-calling is the exact opposite of what Scripture tells us to do.

It is never too early to start training our little ones to use their words wisely. Proverbs 18:21 says, "Death and life are in the power of the tongue: and they that love it shall eat the fruit thereof" (KJV). What great power lies in this small member of our bodies—the tongue.

> Likewise, the tongue is a small part of the body, but it makes great boasts. Consider what a great forest is set on fire by a small spark. The tongue also is a fire, a world of evil among the parts of the body. It corrupts the whole person, sets the whole course of his life on fire, and is itself set on fire by hell. (James 3:5–6)

Because the tongue is a fire, in a world of evil, one small word accompanied by a wrong attitude or lack of restraint can kindle hurt, pain, brokenness, and hate. Name-calling and harsh words can bring death to character. God has entrusted humankind, the highest form of life, with the blessed ability to communicate. How are we, God's children, maintaining and nurturing this power? Is our conversation setting others on fire, or warming their hearts?

> Is our conversation setting others on fire, or warming their hearts?

Having bright, flaming red hair as a child, I became the victim of numerous harsh comments.

"Hey, carrottop!"

"Flame on, you're blinding my eyes!"

"Fire engine head! Turn off the heat!"

There were many others—they actually continued through my college years—each one stinging a bit more. I wanted to dye my hair or cut it off, neither option being acceptable to my mother! I had only one course of action—try to keep moving forward.

Had I known Christ, I might have endured the fight as a "good soldier of Christ Jesus" (2 Timothy 2:3), but instead I became a casualty in the battle of name-calling. Low self-esteem and deep-rooted insecurity developed from seemingly harmless words. I didn't die physically, but emotionally parts of me were slowly humiliated.

How many times do we hear children engaging in conversation warfare, degrading one another with rude comments and sharp remarks that sting like a scorpion? Sarcasm tends to be the new rule in language development—satirical remarks uttered with the intent of taunting another. Subtle, chiding comments that certainly do not build up but tear down. It's actually commonplace and completely acceptable in today's culture. Cartoons, television shows, and movies all need to be carefully monitored. Very often, it isn't the words spoken, but the underlying tone of voice or inflection of speech. It seems this conversation warfare begins earlier and earlier, often right after a child begins talking.

> Sarcasm is derived from the Greek, *sarcasmus*, meaning "to pluck off the skin."[2]

"All the popular kids are sarcastic," said J.J. "In order to be popular you have to be sarcastic."

My husband and I teach the seventh-grade boys' Sunday school class at our church. Fourteen strong, lively adolescent boys. Every week is an adventure. In these young boys, I see our future fathers and church leaders which incites great motivation to pray for each one of them.

As we listened to some of them talk, my husband and I challenged the rule of sarcasm—the biting tone of their voice as they spoke to one another. "Do you all know that sarcasm really means 'plucking off the skin'?" I asked. "It's pretty serious stuff."

After an exuberant debate on sarcasm, we asked them to consider the proverb, "The tongue has the power of life and death" (Proverbs 18:21).

"Can you recall a name or comment that was made to you as a child that left a lasting scar and even deep-seated wounds?" we asked.

"Why is sarcasm considered cool? Do you enjoy being degraded by someone's belittling remarks? Do you think that pleases God? Is there anywhere in Scripture that God uses sarcastic remarks? Nowhere at all. For to God, 'Pleasant words are a honeycomb, sweet to the soul and healing to the bones'" (Proverbs 16:24).

"Consider in your own life words that have given you life, hope, and a reason to persevere. Perhaps it was one of your teachers who sparked purpose in you, giving you vision for your future. Perhaps your father or mother encouraged you in some gift, talent, attribute, or spiritual gifting. God gives the gifts of edification, encouragement, and wisdom for the purpose of enlarging the heart. All we ask is that you think about this. We challenge you to be the one who stands against sarcastic communication. Be bold. Walk away," I urged.

Who knows whether we made an impact, but creating awareness by modeling healthy communication patterns ensures success—even if it comes years later. Dr. Patricia Morgan writes, "The next generation will not be fathered by persuasive pulpiteers and public orators, but by committed adults

"Silence. Speaking up. Both change destinies. When we use these tools inappropriately, we can do great harm. And when we use them as God intended, we can change our world for the better."[3]

who will spend quality time with them, imparting life both by instruction and by example."[4]

Guidelines for Conversations in Our Homes

While searching the writings of Amy Carmichael, missionary to India, I came across five powerful watchwords that I have since implemented as guidelines for the conversations in our home. Before any conversation, she suggests asking the following questions:

- "Is it true?
- Is it kind?
- Is it necessary?
- Does it (the conversation) build the other person up?
- And then, in our dealings with others, is it 'Never *about*; always *to*'?"[5] (If we find ourselves hurt or offended by someone—we go to him or her first.)

In *The Shaping of a Christian Family*, Elisabeth Elliot poses the question, "What does family love look like?" She refers to Paul's words:

[Be] like-minded, having the same love, being one in spirit and purpose. Do nothing out of selfish ambition or vain conceit, but in humility consider others better than yourselves. Each of you should look not only to your own interests, but also to the interests of others. Your attitude should be the same as that of Christ Jesus: Who, being in very nature God, did not consider equality with God something to be grasped, but made himself nothing, taking the very nature of a servant. (Philippians 2:2–7)

All members of a family, each uniquely designed and fashioned with individual personalities, must be committed to family unity and daily exercising of this principle: "Build yourselves up in your most holy faith and pray in the Holy Spirit. Keep yourselves in God's love as you wait for the mercy of our Lord Jesus Christ to bring you to eternal life" (Jude 20–21).

As parents, we must model and train our children in good communication skills. The Word of God is the best training manual I can find, full of promises, hope, and answers to our real-life questions. It proves to be an incredible tool for holding one another accountable. "The Holy Scriptures may be learned by children as soon as they are capable of understanding anything," writes Charles Spurgeon.

> It is a very remarkable fact, which I have heard asserted by many teachers, that children will learn to read out of the Bible better than from any book. From a very child, Timothy had known the sacred writings. This expression is, no doubt, used to show that we cannot begin too early to imbue the minds of our children with Scriptural knowledge. Babes receive impressions long before we are aware of the fact. It soon learns the love of its mother, and its own dependence; and if the mother be wise, it learns the meaning of obedience and the necessity of yielding its will to a higher will. This may be the keynote of its whole future life. If it learns obedience and submission early, it may save a thousand tears from the child's eyes, and as many from the mother's heart.[6]

Years ago, my sarcastic tongue had become a real problem in my marriage and home. I was tired of the tongue lashings, pained looks, and angry words—I knew they were hurting God's heart and my husband. I decided to search the Scriptures for principles regarding our situation. I couldn't escape the truth of how I should be using my words. I started writing Scripture passages, which are now referred to as "The Family Law of Kindness" in my household, on Post-it Notes and sticking them all over our house. This little practice made a big difference.

Just sit for a minute and consider some of the Scripture verses I found. You may even want to grab some Post-it Notes!

Scripture	Family Law of Kindness
Proverbs 10:11	The mouth of the righteous is a fountain of life.
Proverbs 16:24	Pleasant words are a honeycomb, sweet to the soul.
Proverbs 10:19	He who holds his tongue is wise.
Proverbs 10:31	The mouth of the righteous brings forth wisdom.
Proverbs 16:23	A wise man's heart guides his mouth.
Proverbs 21:23	He who guards his mouth and his tongue keeps himself from calamity.
Proverbs 12:18	The tongue of the wise brings healing.
Proverbs 16:21	Pleasant words promote instruction.

(Continued)

Scripture	Family Law of Kindness
Proverbs 17:27	A man of knowledge uses words with restraint.
Proverbs 4:24	Keep corrupt talk far from your lips.
Proverbs 10:13	Wisdom is found on the lips of the discerning.
Proverbs 10:21	The lips of the righteous nourish many.
Psalm 34:13	Keep your tongue from evil and your lips from speaking lies.
Ephesians 4:29	Do not let any unwholesome talk come out of your mouths; but only what is helpful for building others up according to their needs, that it may benefit those who listen.

My sarcastic tongue held the potential to bring disaster of titanic proportions upon my home and family. Proverbs 12:18 says it all. "Reckless words pierce like a sword." Would I thrust a sword into the heart of a loved one? Of course not. But, this proverb makes it very clear my sarcastic (reckless) tongue holds the same destructive potential as a sword.

I'm saddened when forced to realize that not all children have people in their lives who understand the destructive poten-

"Keep vigilant watch over your heart; *that's* where life starts. Don't talk out of both sides of your mouth; avoid careless banter, white lies, and gossip. Keep your eyes straight ahead; ignore all sideshow distractions. Watch your step, and the road will stretch out smooth before you." (Proverbs 4:23–26 MSG)

tial of the tongue. While standing in line at the checkout counter of a local grocery store, I met little Abby. I kept being drawn to this little girl who was with her daddy. He was purchasing an alcoholic beverage and smelled as though he had already consumed a bit before making this purchase. My heart began to swell with compassion toward this child.

"What's your name?" I asked her quietly.

"Abby," she smiled.

"Yeah, now tell her your *reeee-aaaa-l name*," her daddy smugly remarked. "We call her dumb—."

Stunned, I tried to remain composed, refusing to look his way. Leaning down, I looked into Abby's eyes and whispered, "Well, Abby is a beautiful name," thinking to myself, *I believe Abigail means "Father's Joy."* Taking a slow, deep breath, I looked at Abby's father and said, "Sir, please don't say that to this precious child. She is very special."

He grunted and mumbled under his breath.

I left burdened, and prayed protection over Abby. "What will happen to little Abby, Lord?" I prayed. Planted in soil that lacks the proper nutrients for healthy growth, she will need God.

A few days later, while sitting in Barnes and Noble, I watched a mother yell at her daughter, "You pig! You're disgusting!"—all because the little girl had burped out loud by accident. I watched the whole thing. Don't worry, I restrained myself this time, closing my eyes and lifting up a silent prayer.

I can't help but wonder, "What will happen to these children when they grow up? Will they be caught in the same cycle of negativity and abuse? Will they be able to rise above the harsh, reckless words that have been spoken to and around them? What would they be like if they were in different circumstances? Is their potential being nurtured and cultivated? I'm afraid not, but God knows the very number of hairs on their heads and will be there for them.

When I find myself in these situations, I am greatly challenged. You see, none of us is a perfect parent or caregiver; we all "fall short of the glory of God" (Romans 3:23). Yet, I realize that it is my responsibility, even my calling, to unlock the creative and spiritual potential in my children and those I am responsible to care for.

> Above all, love each other deeply, because love covers over a multitude of sins.
> (1 Peter 4:8)

As an active member of my church, I make a commitment at every child's baptism to assist the parents in the spiritual formation of their child. While fulfilling this commitment in the nursery, I often receive glimpses into each child's developing character. I can't quit smiling when I am on duty as a worker in the Runners Room (three- and four-year-olds).

When the rocking horse's leg fell off, Hannah, a dear four-year-old girl with big, brown eyes, held my face in her hands and assured me, "It's gonna be okay." I saw a compassionate young woman in her little eyes, helping the body of Christ one day through painful situations. Somehow, her comfort reached deep down inside my soul and made me feel better.

"Yes, Hannah, I believe it will be okay," I smiled. "Thank you for your kind words."

Author Cheri Fuller writes,

Just as children have critical windows of opportunity for learning language, music, and logic, they also have important spiritual windows of opportunity. These windows are pathways to your children's hearts during the growing up years, when their hearts and minds are most open to experiencing the wonder of God's creation, coming to know him and his ways through the Bible, talking and listening to him through prayer, serving him, and participating in the church community. It is essential, however, that parents start early. The early years are the time when the child is most receptive to spiritual nurturing and training.[7]

Pediatricians agree that toddlers are capable of understanding one hundred to two hundred words. If a toddler can understand a hundred words or more, why not make those one hundred or more words positive, powerful, and packed full of potential? Moses tells us exactly how to do this in Deuteronomy 6:1–25, which I call "The Deuteronomy 6 Mandate." Take time read to this passage of Scripture, especially noting verses 5–9:

> Love the LORD your God with all your heart and with all your soul and with all your strength. These commandments that I give you today are to be upon your hearts. Impress them on your children. Talk about them when you sit at home and when you walk along the road, when you lie down and when you get up. Tie them as symbols on your hands and bind them on your foreheads. Write them on the doorframes of your houses and on your gates.

Note the active verbs in this passage: love, impress, talk, tie, and write. Herein lies Moses' charge to the people of Israel concerning the methodology of child development and personal communication within a family. From my interpretation of this mandate, I see the training to be a full-time occupation—twenty-four hours a day!

- First and foremost, we must love God more than anything else in the world.
- God's Word must, and I repeat, *must* be the standard in our homes. We must, as parents, impress upon our children our love for God and his Word.

- More is caught than taught, remember? So, our children must see us living out God's principles on a day-to-day, minute-by-minute basis. But note, this doesn't mean being perfect—it means being mature followers of Christ, who make mistakes, ask for forgiveness, and daily lean on a God who is big and powerful.
- We must talk about God and his Word during our entire day—every day of the week, not just Sundays.

You might ask, "How in the world do I make that happen?" Well, as discussed earlier, you must daily evaluate your own behavior, modeling to your children godly character. As Abraham Herschel so wisely spoke, "What we need more than anything else is not textbooks but text people. It is the personality of the teacher which is the text that the pupils read, the text that they will never forget."

The Deuteronomy 6 Mandate says it all. Parents are to walk, talk, breathe, live, move, and be to our children, text people for God. They will copy the tone and inflection of our voices, reflect our countenances, develop the same method of communication we exhibit, and grow up imitating what they saw in the home.

Now that my children are older, I see the foundational teachings in full operation. When they were young, I thought I was talking to the walls. But I kept talking! I knew somehow, somewhere, someday, it would all sink in.

Consistency and repetition are two of the greatest teaching tools. "One of the frequent obstacles to spiritual development is the lack of continuity that children experience. Perhaps we start to move down a track of training but fail to finish the course. Maybe we examine the facts of a Bible story with our kids but fail to discuss the personal implications of the story's principles. Sometimes we encourage and applaud certain behavior from our kids for a period of time, but after a while we become oblivious or distracted and stop reinforcing that activity, thus sending a mixed message."[8]

The greatest enemy of consistency is weariness. I have no doubt that you know what it means to be weary! Weariness usually wraps its ugly arms around parents about 4:00 or 5:00 p.m., right around dinnertime. Your patience has been exhausted. Your mind is dulled and potentially becoming a bit cloudy by this hour. Walking in weariness for any length of time is a dangerous place. Several years ago, I was diagnosed with fibromyalgia, a condition with a plethora of symptoms—one being chronic fatigue. Already afflicted with osteoarthritis, *this* diagnosis and the onset of fatigue were overwhelming to me. Number one, I didn't want to believe I had fibromyalgia and number two, I hated the fatigue. Having always been an energetic, high-powered, goal-oriented individual, this stopped me dead in my tracks.

As mothers and fathers, we must take care of ourselves and be sure we are operating from a full tank of emotional, physical, and spiritual strength. Day in and day out the mundane melody of life drones on and can potentially discourage and even disable us. I can vividly remember days when I would sit down in the midst of my three little ones and cry out loud, "I can't take anymore. Oh, God, help me! I am so-o-o-o tired!" Even today, with three active teenagers—or "young adults," as I prefer to call them—I find myself battling fatigue and weariness. How do I remain consistent when these enemies try to

"Fatigue is different from drowsiness. Drowsiness tends to be simply the feeling of a need for sleep while fatigue involves loss of energy and motivation as well. Drowsiness and apathy (a feeling of indifference or not caring about what happens) can often accompany fatigue."[9]

overcome me? I believe that is why Scripture offers me so much encouragement in this area.

Scripture Concerning Our Weariness and Fatigue	Scriptural Relief for Weariness and Fatigue
Matthew 11:28 "Come to me, all you who are weary . . ."	Matthew 11:28, 29 ". . . and I will give you rest. Take my yoke upon you and learn from me." Key: Learn from God.
Galatians 6:9 "Let us not become weary in doing good . . ." Key: Do not give up.	Galatians 6:9 ". . . for at the proper time we will reap a harvest if we do not give up."
Hebrews 12:3 "When we become weary and lose heart, we must . . ." (author translation)	Hebrews 12:3 ". . . consider him who endured such opposition from sinful men." Key: Consider what Jesus endured.
Psalm 142:6 "Listen to my cry, for I am in desperate need."	Jeremiah 31:25 "I will refresh the weary and satisfy the faint." Key: God will refresh and satisfy.
Matthew 26:41 "The spirit is willing, but the body is weak."	Isaiah 50:4 "The Sovereign LORD has given me an instructed tongue, to know the word that sustains the weary. He wakens me morning by morning, wakens my ear to listen like one being taught." Key: Listen to God. Know his Word.

The power of Scripture has carried me through many a day. As I have been reading through my journals in preparing for the writing of this book, I have been overwhelmed at the volume of Scriptures I have recorded over the past twenty years. These Scriptures have been both a lifeline and an anchor in helping me remain consistent in the daily routine—or at least try to remain consistent.

Being consistent doesn't mean your home and schedule must be inflexible, it means you establish a regular pattern of activity that makes your children feel secure and stable. Think of your consistency as the warm blanket that wraps your family every day and fosters nurture, routine, and a sense of order. It is a good thing.

Years ago, I wrote a simple little praise tune that my children could easily remember and hide in their hearts based on Proverbs 16:24: "Pleasant words are a honeycomb, sweet to the soul and healing to the bones."

Prior to teaching them this little chorus, we gathered together at our family altar and read Proverbs 16:24 together. After reading it, we went into the kitchen. On the counter I had placed a little bowl of honey, a lemon, and freshly baked bread. I drizzled the bread with honey and let my little ones taste and see how sweet this little bit of honey tastes.

"Delicious, isn't it?" I would ask.

"Mmmm. Can I have more?" they chimed in.

"We'll see. Tell me, Brooke, is this honey sweet or sour?"

"It's very sweet and yummy!" she smiled.

"Now, let's take this nice, plump lemon and squeeze its juice on our bread."

"How does that taste, Grant?"

With puckered lips he remarked, "Sour! Yuck!"

"Yes, it is very sour," I agreed. "God says that pleasant words are sweet like honey to everyone around us. But, when we speak unkind words to someone, it is like they're tasting bitter lemon. We want to do our best to speak pleasant words that build others up."

Proverbs 10:11 says, "The mouth of the righteous is a fountain of life." As you can see, it is critical to begin early in training the tongues of our children to be fountains of life—not stagnant pools or dismal swamps of unkindness and cruelty. As your children become accustomed to listening to their words and the words of others, realizing the power that the tongue holds, changes will occur in their hearts. "A word aptly spoken is like apples of gold in settings of silver" (Proverbs 25:11). Let's all enjoy a rock-solid family atmosphere where members build one another up, not tear one another down!

Time in the Tower

Training the Tongue

1. What grabbed your attention in this chapter? Is there one specific area you feel the need to think more about? Open your journal and talk to God about it. Ask him to help you begin the "relearning" process.

2. Read Deuteronomy 6:5–9. Consider ways you can talk to your children about God and his Word. Ask God for opportunities throughout the day to talk about him. May I once more recommend Kenneth Taylor's classic work, *The Bible in Pictures for Little Eyes*, and all his devotional classics:

   Right Choices (Carol Stream, IL: Tyndale House, 1999)

   Family Time Bible (Carol Stream, IL: Tyndale House, 2003)

   Big Thoughts for Little People (Carol Stream, IL: Tyndale House, 1990)

   Stories about Jesus (Carol Stream, IL: Tyndale Kids, 1994)

   Giant Steps for Little People (Carol Stream, IL: Tyndale Kids, 1985)

   Good News for Little People (Carol Stream, IL: Tyndale Kids, 1991)

Wise Words for Little People (Carol Stream, IL: Tyndale House, 1987)

3. Today is a "hands-on" day. Review "The Family Law of Kindness" in this chapter. Be creative and post these "laws" in obvious places around the house. Use Post-it Notes or index cards. Begin memorizing these and teaching them to your children. Transform these beautiful Scriptures into prayer:
   - "Lord, help me hold my tongue today. This is the wise thing to do."
   - "Lord, do not let any, and I mean *any*, unwholesome talk come out of my mouth."
   - "Help me, Lord, to build up my children."
   - "May what I say to my spouse today be helpful and beneficial."

Notes

1. Elisabeth Elliot, *The Shaping of a Christian Family* (Grand Rapids, MI: Fleming H. Revell, 1992), 172.

2. MSN Encarta Dictionary, http://encarta.msn.com/dictionary_/sarcasm.html.

3. Dr. Michael D. Sedler, *When To Speak Up and When To Shut Up* (Grand Rapids, MI: Fleming H. Revell, 2003), 137.

4. Dr. Patricia Morgan, *How to Raise Children of Destiny* (New Kensington, PA: Whitaker House, 2003), Front matter.

5. Amy Carmichael, *God's Missionary* (Fort Washington, PA: Christian Literature Crusade, 1983), 9.

6. Charles Spurgeon, *Come Ye Children: Practical Help Telling Children about Jesus* (Scotland, UK: Christian Focus Publications Ltd., 2003).

7. Cheri Fuller, *Opening Your Child's Spiritual Windows: Ideas to Nurture Your Child's Relationship with God* (Grand Rapids, MI: Zondervan, 2001), 14.

8. George Barna, *Transforming Children into Spiritual Champions: Why Children Should Be Your Church's #1 Priority* (Ventura, CA: Regal Books, 2003), 91–92.

9. MedLine Plus, "Medical Encyclopedia: Fatigue," http://www.nlm.nih.gov/medlineplus/ency/article/003088.htm.

GRACE
There's a Message inside Every Mess

> "The lesson is one of deep import: the only humility that is really ours is not that which we try to show before God in prayer, but that which we carry with us, and carry out, in our ordinary conduct; the insignificances of daily life are the importance and the tests of eternity, because they prove what really is the spirit that possesses us. It is in our most unguarded moments that we really show and see what we are. To know the humble man, to know how the humble man behaves, you must follow him in the common course of daily life."[1]

Oh, I don't want this day to end. It has been absolutely perfect," I told Rob.

While packing up our beach gear, I inhaled a final dose of ocean air. Earlier in the day we had found an incredible stretch of uninhabited beach—a long stretch of solitude—as we were driving along the coastline.

"Let's stop here and check this out," Rob grinned.

The discovery was one of life's little surprises, when God shines upon a day and all seems perfect. Days such as these are rare, but I've learned to receive them with much gratitude, making every minute rich and fulfilling. I decided to take a walk—alone—stealing a few minutes of much-needed, undivided time with God. The past year had been a tough one, due to health challenges. As I walked, I felt miles away from the drains of daily life with its chronic pain, tensions, distractions, and busyness. Solitude embraced me and held me with passion and love. I felt so close to God, all my cares being swept into the water and carried out to sea. The sand was smooth as silk, highly unusual for the North Carolina coast. It was so easy to walk on, solid and stable under my feet.

I felt the still, small voice call to me, so I sat down on the warm sand. The glistening foam of the crashing waves covered me like a bubble bath. "I am with you in all your pain, my daughter. Follow me closely and I will make the way smooth."

I answered by writing in the sand, for I remembered how Jesus had done that (see John 8:1–11). All I could write was, *I will.* Two little words of surrender.

I hated to leave this glorious reprieve, this little pause from life, but it was time to go. As we drove away from this stretch of solitude—this isolated perfect day—I left a little piece of my soul in the sand. A wonderful divine exchange had occurred—my weakness for his power.

Paul knows all about the divine exchange.

Because of the extravagance of those revelations, and so I wouldn't get a big head, I was given the gift of a handicap to keep me in constant touch with my limitations. Satan's angel did his best to get me down; what he in fact did was push me to my knees. No danger then of walking around high and mighty! At first I didn't think of it as a gift, and begged God to remove it. Three times I did that, and then he told me, My

"It is a blessed position to which the providence of God reduces us when we find ourselves face-to-face with an over-mastering necessity. We confess that we are not sufficient in ourselves; but our sufficiency is from God. We cannot make a revival; or save a soul; or convince a heart of sin, or break it down in contrition; we cannot comfort, or counsel, or satisfy the parching thirst. And when we have reached the end of self, we have got to the beginning of God."[2]

grace is enough; it's all you need. My strength comes into its own in your weakness. Once I heard that, I was glad to let it happen. I quit focusing on the handicap and began appreciating the gift. It was a case of Christ's strength moving in on my weakness. Now I take limitations in stride, and with good cheer, these limitations that cut me down to size—abuse, accidents, opposition, bad breaks. I just let Christ take over! And so the weaker I get, the stronger I become." (2 Corinthians 12:7–10 MSG)

Affliction had wreaked havoc on Paul's life. After shipwrecks, stonings, imprisonment, all kinds of verbal abuse, and more, Paul had no natural strength left. A man of great natural gifting and talent (see Galatians 1:11–24) brought to his knees. Every moment of suffering brought him closer and closer to the realization of his need for grace. Paul was brought to the end of himself. I believe, if Paul were alive today, we would interpret his life as a mess. A big spiritual mess.

"Poor Paul, did you hear what happened to him today?" Fran told Debbie. "We need to pray."

"No, tell me," said Debbie.

"Well, he was shipwrecked . . . again! Isn't this the third time? Wasn't he in another shipwreck last month? I wonder what is wrong with Paul. It's one thing after another."

"Who knows? He's sure having a tough time. He must be doing something wrong. Didn't he get bit by a snake, too? What's up with that?" Debbie asked.

"He's obviously doing too much or hanging around with the wrong people."

But, little do Debbie and Fran know, tucked inside the mess of Paul's life was a life-changing message from a God who loves him very much: "My grace is enough . . . My strength comes into its own in your weakness."

Amid all the chaotic circumstances surrounding Paul, he became well acquainted with the gift of God's grace. His life may have looked like a mess on the outside, but on the inside he was becoming a rock. Grace is never earned by human effort— quite the contrary. It is given in times of weakness or inadequacy. "Grace is the enabling," observes author Bob Sorge, "that supersedes all human inadequacies."[3] To me, grace is the hand that holds me up. Without it, I'd fall flat on my face.

Grace may be defined as "appropriately, the free, unmerited love and favor of God, the spring and source of all the benefits men receive from him."[4] Like Paul, our families need the gift of grace. Day in and day out. The family routine can, and

> "Grace, then, is God's favor freely given to those who do not deserve this favor."[5]

I stress can, be daunting in its daily demands. The perfect days on a sunny beach are rare. Quite frankly, the twenty-four hour cycle of "things to be done, things to be undone, and things to be redone" can be, at times, overwhelming. I wish it weren't true. But, it is. Therefore, we need the gift of grace to be in full operation in our homes.

The spring and source of grace is God. He clearly defines his enabling grace throughout the Scriptures. Let's look at three specific areas:

1. Moments of Grace: This is grace for everyday life.
2. Seasons of Grace: This is grace for special circumstances.
3. A Legacy of Grace: Each moment added to each season produces the sum of a life lived in grace.

Moments of Grace

I always see double and experience bouts of blurred vision when remembering the preschool years of my three children: Candace, now twenty-one and in her final year of college, and our twins, Brooke and Grant, seventeen and in their last year of high school.

Twins. Yes, God saw fit to bless my husband and me with twins! The day we brought our double blessing home from the hospital, Candace was celebrating her fourth birthday. Not only did I have to recover from the delivery, I became immediate hostess to her "everything pink" birthday party. Adorned with a pink party hat, I should have realized that life, as I had previously known it, would never be the same. This was just the beginning of learning the beautiful truths of John 15:12–13: "My command is this: Love each other as I have loved you. Greater love has no one than this, that he lay down his life for his friends" (which, I add, includes family).

Over the next few years, this Scripture became literal in meaning. I don't think I slept for almost a year, feeling as though I might not survive life's daily demands. I vividly remember my first time out to the mall with all three children. Countless older women stopped me, cooing and oooh-ing over the twins, congratulating big sister, and commenting, "Honey, I don't know how you do it. Twins. I couldn't handle one child, let alone two at one time."

My response? "By the grace of God. Only the grace of God gets me through the day. Minute by minute, I ask for grace. I give God all the credit!"

Every day my natural strength declined. They had ear infections, food allergies—double everything. I learned about limitations for the first time in my life. I realized I couldn't do everything on my own anymore; I was in over my head.

In many ways, those were the best days of my life—full of surprises, simple delights, times of uproarious laughter, and precious memories. I learned to live one day at a time. Sometimes one hour at a time. The words from my journal, dated January 29, 1990, illustrate this:

> My day began hearing these words on a radio show: "There is nothing little to a father in the thing that troubles his little child . . . and your great God will not think that you intrude upon Him if you bring your daily troubles to Him."

I had responded to this by writing,

> Presently, my life is very daily. Very mundane, ordinary, and daily. Minute precluding minute—an orchestra of minutes— each one resounding a peculiar note—hopefully blending and unifying into blissful harmony. Yet, realistically, I know there are always going to be times of discord, flatness, and often shrillness. Not every minute blends, yet my hope is that the Master Conductor will orchestrate it all unto perfection. If I didn't have this hope and trust in God's infinite ability, I would be totally lost.

I wrote those words seventeen years ago. Where has time gone? All the individual minutes have become the deep well of memories from which my children and I drink.

In music, a grace note is a note of embellishment, usually written small. The grace note, of no consequence on its own, when added to the whole work makes the composition lovelier. Moments of grace, then, add to the composition of our days, making them lovelier. Without grace notes in my symphony of minutes, I would be a mess.

> "Annoyance is a feeling of irritation or feelings of mild anger and impatience."[6]

Moments of grace can be antidotes to all the little irritants of daily life. In *The Screwtape Letters,* C. S. Lewis affectionately calls irritants "pinpricks." Screwtape, the senior demon, advises Wormwood, his nephew and apprentice, "to build up in that house a good settled habit of mutual annoyances . . . send daily pinpricks."[7] Screwtape wants the Christian to fall. There will be daily pinpricks sent to annoy and hinder your family's unity. Mark this down: The devil does not want your household to be peaceful—ever! He hates peace, unity, cohesion—anything that promotes God and his kingdom. So, be ready for him. Grab a grace note from God—I've given you a few below:

Moments of grace operate when we can . . .	Grace Notes from God
overlook an offense.	Proverbs 17:9 "He who covers over an offense promotes love, but whoever repeats the matter separates close friends."
forgive as we have been forgiven.	Colossians 3:13 "Bear with each other and forgive whatever grievances you may have against one another. Forgive as the Lord forgave you."

(Continued)

Moments of grace operate when we can . . .	Grace Notes from God
speak the truth in love.	Ephesians 4:15 "Instead, speaking the truth in love, we will in all things grow up into him who is the Head, that is, Christ."
be slow to speak and slow to anger.	James 1:19–20 "My dear brothers, take note of this: Everyone should be quick to listen, slow to speak and slow to become angry, for man's anger does not bring about the righteous life that God desires."
laugh at ourselves.	James 1:2–3 "Consider it pure joy, my brothers, whenever you face trials of many kinds, because you know that the testing of your faith develops perseverance."
successfully handle conflict.	Galatians 5:16–18 "So I say, live by the Spirit, and you will not gratify the desires of the sinful nature. For the sinful nature desires what is contrary to the Spirit, and the Spirit what is contrary to the sinful nature.

(Continued)

Moments of grace operate when we can . . .	Grace Notes from God
	They are in conflict with each other, so that you do not do what you want. But if you are led by the Spirit, you are not under law."
calmly handle emergencies or interruptions, such as a broken-down car, sick child, bloody nose, etc.	Psalm 119:165 "Great peace have they who love your law, and nothing can make them stumble."

All these things come, one by one, with the promise that God is our source and supply and that his grace will be sufficient. We will all have bad days, when we are impatient, overwhelmed, unmotivated, exhausted, sick and tired, depressed, etc. But as we acquire and apply moments of grace, the bad days will not win. The bad days will not leave a lasting mark on our homes. The disastrous effects of a bad day will decrease as the character of God increases in our lives. Hopefully, as we grow in grace, our homes will become fortresses of faith—brick by spiritual brick.

Seasons of Grace

Sustaining grace. This is grace for the long haul. Difficulty. Struggle. Special circumstances. All for the purpose of growing in maturity. "Sustain" is derived from the Latin root *sustineo*, a combination of *sus-* and *tenere*, "to hold up."[8] God's grace promises to sustain us when we are under a heavy strain. He will uphold us (see Psalm 119:116–17); he will keep us from sinking into despondency (see Psalm 40:2); he will give power and great ability (2 Corinthians 12:9; Acts 4:33); he will give more grace (James 4:6).

Nature always reflects spiritual truth. Imagine learning a lesson about grace from seaweed that is found in the depths of the ocean. It is said about seaweed that it

> copes with mechanical stress by having a strong holdfast. Unlike land plants, seaweed lacks roots, leaves, and stems, but has other specialized structures. Instead of roots, seaweed has a holdfast, which helps it stay firmly fixed to rocks. At the end of the holdfast is a tiny disc, which secretes extremely powerful glue. Try pulling seaweed from a rock and discover how effective this glue can be. Instead of leaves, seaweed has a blade or series of branching fronds growing from the holdfast. Like leaves from seed-producing plants, the blades and fronds are the photosynthesizing, or food-producing, parts of the plant.[9]

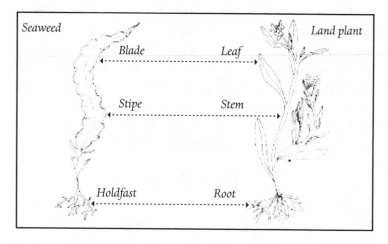

During a season of grace, we need an extremely powerful glue to keep us rooted and grounded, to help us maintain some sense of sanity. Grace is that glue.

Noah's deliverance from the flood was to be the introduction of a new age—the first great act of God's redeeming

grace on behalf of a sinful world. In it, God manifested
the great principles of grace: mercy in the midst of judgment; life through death; faith as a means of deliverance;
and the one channel through which the blessing comes.
The family was the instrument through which sin acquired
its universal dominion. This principle was not to be res-
cued from the power of sin and to be adopted into the
covenant of grace. The family would not serve as a tool to
establish the kingdom of God. The relationship of parents
and children had been the means for transmitting and
establishing the power of sin. Now the family was to
become the vehicle for the extension of the Kingdom of
God's grace. God always gives grace in proportion to the
duty he imposes.[10]

Digest those last words for just a moment: "God always
gives grace in proportion to the duty he requires."

In 1990, my father was diagnosed with cancer of the head
and neck. On September 10th he underwent a six-and-a-half-
hour radical surgery. The surgical team removed part of his
tongue, a tumor in his throat, part of his mandible bone, and
several lymph nodes in his neck.

"It's going to be a long road with radiation and difficult
dietary restrictions, but he made it through," the doctors said.
"We can offer no guarantees, only hope."

By this time, I had been married six years, Candace was
four, and the twins, Brooke and Grant, were a little over eight
weeks old. Needless to say, time was of the essence. My father
and I spent a great deal of time talking and being together. This
time in my life was a season of grace. I needed grace for the
long haul—three years, to be exact.

In July of 1993, his time was coming to an end. The last
days in the hospital were intense, yet miraculous. On July 4th, I
wrote, "Here I sit in the hospital room with my Dad. As I sit by

his bed, in the final hours of his life, I know the power of forgiveness is real and true. Hate has been washed away by the blood of Jesus. I finally have a relationship with my Dad and he has to die. All I ask, God, is that it not be today. Today is my sister's birthday. It would not be good if he died today. Please give him a few more days." God answered.

I left the hospital for a few hours and returned later that day with my sister. My dad was sitting up in his bed, as if he'd never been sick. Standing in amazement, I knew God had something very special planned. The next few hours were a birthday present from God. We talked. We laughed. The hospital corpsman wheeled his bed in front of the big, picturesque window facing the harbor so that we could all watch the Fourth of July fireworks display. Together, the three of us watched the most beautiful fireworks ever. Words can't express the deep gratitude I felt as I saw a real-life miracle unfold.

"God, you are so good," I silently prayed. "You care about every minute detail of our lives. How can I ever thank you?"

Two days later, something happened. It was close to midnight. My sister and I were once again sitting at my father's bedside. His Fourth of July reprise of health was short-lived and once again he was incoherent.

Suddenly, he opened his eyes and began talking. Obviously, we perked up and realized he was conversing with someone. He kept directing his gaze and words to the corner of the room. I thought he was hallucinating, but the conversation continued.

"Yes, Sir, I am ready! I'm ready to go! I want to go now. Yes, Sir!" said my dad.

Then, the quiet. I assumed someone was talking to him.

"Yes, don't forget my son Michael, he's in the Navy. He is in Philadelphia. Yes, Sir. Don't forget my son."

Quiet again. Then, he began to bellow in laughter. Bellow. He laughed like I'd never seen him laugh. It was unbelievable. I looked at my sister. She looked at me. We sat stunned and perplexed. Finally, he quieted down. I touched his arm, got real close to his face and looked into his eyes. "Daddy, do you know who this is?" I asked.

"Yes, you're Janell," he replied.

(*Okay*, I thought, *he's not hallucinating.*) "Daddy, to whom were you talking?" I asked.

In his gruff Marine voice, he motioned with his thumb and pointed upward. "HIM!"

I was speechless. Thank God my sister heard him because no one in my family would have believed me. My dad had been talking to God.

In hindsight, I wish I had asked more questions: "What does he look like? Did you see him? Tell me more!" But, at that moment in time, the conversation between God and my dad was private and precious. We were on holy ground. God was present in that room and I knew his work with my dad was done. All I could think about was my dad's laughter—and how I had seen 1 Peter 1:8–9 come alive: "Though you have not seen him, you love him; and even though you do not see him now, you believe in him and are filled with an inexpressible and glorious joy, for you are receiving the goal of your faith, the salvation of your souls."

"Ushered into heaven, full of the joy of the Lord," my journal records, "July 7th. Dad died early this morning at 3:00 a.m. Susan and I decided to leave shortly after Dad's conversation with God. We knew he wouldn't let go with us there. 'His girls,' as he referred to us, left him to fight his last fight. Oh, Lord, it is painful to let go of him—so much of my life has been invested in restoring this relationship. He is with you and I believe you gave me assurance by the angelic visitation of your presence. He was so happy."

Shortly after his death, I arrived at the hospital to be with my mother. The nurse told me his death was unexpectedly peaceful. She said he should have suffered, but he took one short breath and went to sleep. All praise and glory to God! "Now to him who is able to do immeasurably more than we can ask or imagine, according to his power that is at work within us, to him be glory in the church and in Christ Jesus throughout all generations, for ever and ever!" (Ephesians 3:20–21).

Prior to his death, Dad had asked me to thank all his buddies at the funeral for their love toward him. I promised I would relay the message. So at his funeral, I delivered his words and was able to share the message of Christ. His priest said he knew "Harry is guarding the streets of gold—that is his new assignment. All polished up in his Marine Corps uniform!" Somehow, I thought, that is exactly where he is. I can't wait to dance down those streets one day in heaven—my father and I.

The face of your season of grace will differ from mine. When your difficulties come, and they will, they come with the divine promise that God is the source and supply—and his grace will be sufficient. Sometimes, trials go on and on. I wish they didn't, but they do. When the days turn into months that turn into years, hold fast to the Lord. He will keep you rooted and grounded.

A Legacy of Grace

Each moment added to each season produces the sum of a life lived in grace:

MOMENTS OF GRACE + SEASONS OF GRACE =
    A LEGACY OF GRACE

Andrew Murray writes,

> The concept of grace is one that Christians experience each day of their lives, whether they realize it or not. It's the audacious but biblical idea that we can have a personal relationship

with a holy, eternal God that requires no work on our part, only accepting for ourselves the work of Jesus Christ. Even though our wrongdoing should result in lethal punishment, we are offered forgiveness and life—a second chance to go out there and get it right. The outrageous gift of grace is not to be hoarded, but it is to be extended in all our relationships.[11]

Families thrive in a home environment where grace permeates each room. Our children need to have the grace of God extended to them so they may have a safe environment—a sacred refuge from the world that buffets them daily—in which to grow to maturity. For years I have told my children, "The world on the other side of the threshold of our home is evil enough. Our home should be different. Our home should be a place of safe lodging and restoration. Our home should be filled with a gracious, accepting atmosphere. Before you come in the door, wipe the dust of this world off your feet. Leave it outside" (see Luke 10:10–12).

Several years ago, my children saw these words come to life. Our UPS driver perpetually left our packages crooked against the outside of our garage door—no matter what the weather condition, be it a downpour, a snowstorm, or 100 degrees in the shade. Finally, I ran outside one day to try to ask him if he could please leave them on the front porch, which was covered and therefore protected from the elements.

"I can't cross the threshold, ma'am," he roared, while walking away from me.

Running after him, I cried out, "Sir, could you please stop for a moment. I need to talk to you."

Without a moment's hesitation, he completely ignored me and drove away. *I can't believe it,* I thought. Time after time, the situation repeated itself. Finally, completely exasperated, I yelled, "Why can't you stop? The other UPS man was great—brought the packages right to the front door."

"I can't cross the threshold, ma'am."

That's all he would say. With three children watching my reaction, I crumbled under this man's evil presence.

Several days later, it hit me like a ton of bricks. When the concrete was laid for our driveway, my husband etched the letters "Psalm 127" right at the entrance, the threshold, of our garage. It was here, at this threshold, the UPS driver would leave our packages. His words, "I can't cross the threshold," rang in my ears.

"Kids, come here! I've got it! Guess what? He can't cross our threshold—because evil can't come near our household! God's angels are all around our property, protecting us from evil trespassers!"

It became crystal clear to me that God wouldn't allow this man's evil nature to come anywhere near the sacred refuge of our home. Suddenly, I realized how great God's power really is—an unseen force that is constantly working on our behalf.

> Grace changes a bad situation into a bearable one.

As we've said, grace is an antidote for sharp tongues, harsh words, belittling comments and looks, useless chatter, approaching evil, and idle negativity. It is the glue that holds our family love together. Without grace, our homes would be a war zone.

Fathers and mothers, you must "grow in the grace and knowledge of [y]our Lord and Savior Jesus Christ" (2 Peter 3:18) and "lavish" God's grace on [y]our children (Ephesians 1:7). Amid all the messes of life—and there will be many messes— grace changes a bad situation into a bearable one. Time and time again, I've seen friends and family held by the tender hands of grace. I never grow weary watching the gift of grace soften the lines on a worried brow, quiet the whimpers of a weeping friend, lighten the gravity of a dark situation, or sustain the arms that are weakening under the strain of life. Grace's warm, welcoming presence is what will help you rest in God, trusting that somehow, somewhere, he will show you the message inside every mess.

Time in the Tower

There's a Message inside Every Mess!

1. Read Romans 4:18–21. As you read, highlight the following sentences:

   • Against all hope, . . . in hope . . .
   • Without weakening in his faith, . . .
   • He faced the fact that his body was good as dead.
   • He did not waver through unbelief regarding the promise of God.
   • [He] was strengthened in his faith.
   • [He] gave glory to God.
   • [He was] fully persuaded that God had the power to do what he had promised.

   A simple question must be asked here: "How in the world is this possible?" How did Abraham persevere in this trial? Is it possible he leaned hard on God's promises and God gave him the grace necessary for this season? Spend time today reflecting on a situation in your life, one that perhaps requires the same steadfastness as Abraham's. Pray 2 Corinthians 9:8 over your situation.

2. You've discovered a beautiful spiritual truth from nature—the holdfast of seaweed—in this chapter. Think about a time when life forced you to "hold fast" to God. How did

you stay firmly fixed to the Rock? What was the "extremely powerful glue" that kept you clinging to the Rock?

Notes

1. Andrew Murray, "Humility." World Invisible. http://www .worldinvisible.com/library/murray/5F00.0565/5f00.0565.c.htm.

2. F. B. Meyer, *Moses* (Fort Washington, PA: Christian Literature Crusade, 1994), 102–03.

3. Bob Sorge, *The Fire of Delayed Answers* (Greenwood, MO: Oasis House, 1998).

4. Noah Webster, *An American Dictionary of the English Language* (New York: S. Converse, 1828). Facsimile first edition (Chesapeake, VA: Foundation for American Christian Education, 1967 and all subsequent editions).

5. Wayne Grudem, *Systematic Theology* (Grand Rapids, MI: Zondervan, 1994), 200.

6. MSN Encarta Dictionary. http://encarta.msn.com/dictionary _annoyance.html (accessed March 26, 2007).

7. C. S. Lewis, *The Screwtape Letters* (New York: HarperCollins, 1996), 11.

8. Noah Webster, *An American Dictionary of the English Language*.

9. "Algae Art: Make Your Own Seaweed Print." *Fisheries and Oceans Canada.* http://www.glf.dfo-mpo.gc.ca/sci-sci/bysea-enmer/ activities/activities-activities28-e.html (accessed March 26, 2007).

10. Andrew Murray, *Raising Your Children for Christ* (New Kensington, PA: Whitaker House, 1994), 21–23.

11. Ibid.

CREATIVITY
The Fun Factor

> "The sound of roaring laughter is far more contagious than any cough, sniffle, or sneeze. Humor and laughter can cause a domino effect of joy and amusement, as well as set off a number of positive physical effects."[1]
>
> "Inevitably our earliest memory is a creative/imaginative memory. Leonardo da Vinci's first memory was of being in his crib and having the tail of a kite come down and brush his face. He spent the rest of his life trying to fly, both practically, by means of various flying machines and parachutes, and— perhaps more significantly—by means of his amazing art."[2]

After a long walk beside the vibrant North Sea, I finally reached a stopping place where I climbed down the crags and touched the icy blue water. For some reason, the chilled Scottish air and the cool water on my hand brought to mind a story I had read in *A Chance to Die: The Life and Legacy of Amy Carmichael*: "The rocky beach was her favorite playground, where she would lie prone beside its tide pools and gaze and gaze. There were living things in those pools, things which held endless fascination for the child. Her powers of observation were exquisite, her sympathy boundless."³

Amy Carmichael grew up with the rocky beaches of the Irish Sea her playground. She grew up in a culture that encouraged lying beside tide pools—gazing with endless fascination. For a short season, her days were peppered with life-giving experiences that induced wonder, curiosity, and imagination. I didn't want my time on the crags to end. I didn't want to leave the pathway or the North Sea, which was peaceful and placid, but I knew I must. My short season of childlike play ended too soon.

Childhood is a time when God has made the heart tender, carefree, and open and eager to learn new things. "Childhood," wrote Helen Hayes, "is a short season."⁴

Let's do a little supposing.

What are the absolute essentials that I should plan to build into my child's early education schedule? What if my neighbor is sending her little Mary to a traditional preschool, swimming lessons at the YMCA, preschool creative movement class, and T-ball in the spring and soccer in the fall. When is little Mary going to have free time to explore and have creative play? Time to "be"? I'm just curious.

You might respond, "Creative play? Is that really necessary? Isn't it better to have Mary's time fully structured? You know what the experts say—to provide them with ample building blocks, such as the aforementioned activities in order to assure they develop socially, physically, and emotionally? Won't my little one be socially deprived and inept if she stays home with me? I don't want her to be left behind."

Questions such as these have been a thorn in my side for a long time. Over the years, I have observed children getting busier and busier. For seven years I owned and operated a performing arts studio where I taught creative movement classes for numerous preschoolers. We wiggled and giggled. Acted like

"Middle-class children in America are so overscheduled that they have almost no 'nothing time.' They have no time to call on their own resources and be creative. Creativity is making something out of nothing, and it takes time for that to happen. In our efforts to produce Renaissance children who are competitive in all areas, we squelch creativity."[5]

monkeys jumping on a bed. Ran under parachutes and pretended we were caught in a spider web. Their joy was exuberant and contagious. From the opening of my studio in 1991 to its closing in 1998, I saw a dramatic increase in the number of stressed-out children, busy from sunrise to sunset. Statistics confirm this observation. Newspaper columnist Karen MacPherson writes:

> In recent years, many child development experts have voiced increasing concern over the fact that children are accorded little time or encouragement to engage in imaginative play. Too many children are overscheduled with school activities. When children do have time to play, they too often play with a preprogrammed electronic toy or sit in front of a screen—television, computer or hand-held game—responding to a scenario created by someone else.[6]

During a radio interview with Dr. James Dobson, Dr. Archibald Hart, author of *Stress and Your Child*, was asked, "Does the attitude we take as parents have a dramatic effect on our children?" His answer caught my attention:

> We're getting them up in the morning with 'Hurry up. Get ready. I've got to go to work and you've got to go to school. Take a bite and eat quick, hurry, get ready!' Children are

being taught to live at a hectic pace in today's society. The home—the family environment—creates the stress problems that so many children experience later in life. It's in the home, therefore, in the family, that the solution to the problem lies. What we model to our children teaches them the values that will determine whether they're going to live a stressful life or not. Parents are busier than ever these days. Don't use adrenaline to get everything done. Don't sit all tensed up; don't drive the car with your adrenaline surging. When you're angry, resentful or frustrated, your adrenaline is pumping. If tackling that pile of papers or sink of dishes is going to make you angry and frustrated, set it aside; leave the task. Go hug your child; play a game of Monopoly; spend a few minutes thanking God for your home, family and job. Believe me, your children will take notice—and your physical and emotional well-being will improve.[7]

If our children need anything, they need time to "be." In our hurry-and-scurry culture, we have a biblical imperative to train our children to "be still and know that I am God" (Psalm 46:10). Just listen to yourself throughout the day and make note of how many times you say, "Hurry up!" "Come on, we have to go!" "Can't you move any faster?" "Would you please step it up! I have things to do!"

At a stop sign years ago, I had a mommy meltdown. Feeling the pressure to do what all the other moms were doing, I enrolled Candace (four at the time) in a local preschool. *Three hours, three days a week. That will give me nine hours a week. I can put the twins down for a nap and have some mommy time,* I thought.

But getting three-month-old twins fed, dressed in some fashion, and into car seats—all while getting the precocious four-year-old presentable—became an overwhelming task. To make things worse, I had a friend with twins who did everything with ease.

No pressure, Janell, you can handle this. Get a grip, I scolded myself.

Talk about meltdown. That day a normal street sign became a message from God. Call me crazy, but I think it actually talked to me (smile).

"STOP! This is insane," said a little voice. "This was supposed to decrease your stress level, not increase it. Enough is enough. Keep Candace home. Teach her the basics. Nurture her. Leave the rest in God's hands."

Without a minute's hesitation, I turned the car around and went home. That day was the beginning of our homeschooling adventure. Our very own "Princess Snowflake Preschool" opened the next day. Candace and I would sit side by side in a makeshift schoolroom in the corner of our kitchen, learning letters and numbers while Brooke and Grant took their naps. Mommy time was at a minimum, but the emotional atmosphere of our home was worth every bit of sacrifice. Looking back, that Stop sign was a heavenly message that helped initiate a lifetime of balance.

Balance is extremely important in life. It isn't that extracurricular activities are bad—quite the contrary. The question is, "Are you doing too much?" Being a mother of three very active young adults, I am fully aware of the tendencies to overdo. I find myself saying, "Oh, that will look great on your college application. Perfect."

> We want to direct our children, not drive them.

Catching myself, I wince. *Oh, Janell, what did you just say? For heaven's sake, you are falling into the trap.*

Having a solid college application or professional résumé is very important, but you must remember to exercise caution so as not to push your children too hard. You want to direct them, not drive them. Recently, I helped one of my writing students prepare her portfolio for an upcoming college interview. Overwhelmed by a deluge of papers and pictures, I sat down to catch my breath.

Sorting through it all, I said, "Alex, I see three important aspects of your high school career: dance, modeling, and missions. You need to focus on these three things and show the depth of each aspect of your personality."

Slowly, we crafted the story of Alex—picture by picture. Upon finishing, I marveled at the simplicity of the portfolio and the beauty of Alex's life. Wisely, she had invested herself in three specific areas of concentration.

Days later, I received a phone call from Alex. "Guess what! They loved it!" Alex exclaimed. "The admissions counselor said it was one of the best portfolios she had ever seen. I received the highest scholarship! Can you believe it?"

As I hung up the phone, I silently thanked God for Alex. I recalled the first day I met her. She entered my dance studio, at the age of three, armed and ready for her first preschool creative movement class. Alex brought a plethora of questions, a hunger to learn, a calm demeanor, and a quest for creativity that I had not seen before. Seeds of greatness were evident. I knew Alex would move the earth. Now, years later, she is an accomplished dancer and performer who mesmerizes audiences with her beauty and grace. She has spent hundreds of hours in the dance studio, standing silently at the ballet *barre*, training her body to execute the most difficult *adagios*. Her motivation to reach her highest potential as a ballerina has transferred into every arena of life. Those early years in Alex's life—years where creativity and imagination had time to take root—give credence to the philosophy that children need time and space to "be."

A study was done of ninety-one high achievers, some of whom were Nobel Prize winners. The general outcome was that, as children, they had a great deal of down time—time to create things and be totally imaginative. No rigid scheduling of

"Allow adequate periods of recovery from periods of over-stress. Life is always full of things to do, and there will always be periods of intensified stress or excitement. Such times of high arousal should always be followed with times for recovery. We are not supermen or superwomen, just ordinary mortals with bodies that have their limits and demand recovery time from overuse."[8]

activity upon activity. In his thought-provoking book *The Hurried Child: Growing Up Too Fast Too Soon*, David Elkind challenges, "The concept of childhood, so vital to the traditional American way of life, is threatened with extinction in the society we have created. Today's child has become the unwilling, unintended victim of overwhelming stress—the stress borne of rapid, bewildering social change and constantly rising expectations. We do our children harm when we hurry them through childhood."[9]

His challenge definitely makes me think: Is childhood becoming extinct? Are children being rushed to grow up? What is the big hurry?

When Candace was five, I vividly remember stressing out over school placement. We sensed she should go to traditional kindergarten. Opinions were flowing—as I am sure you can relate—and I was becoming very confused. One day after church, my pastor's wife invited me to come over for a visit. As we talked, she challenged me.

"Janell, can't you let her be a happy little girl who loves Jesus?" she meekly said. "What's the big hurry? She will learn to read. She will learn to add. Relax. Let her be little. Let her play and enjoy her very short childhood."

Her wisdom set me free. I took a deep breath and realized I needed to let Candace be a child. Now, her childhood is over.

She is a grown woman on the threshold of life. Thank God I listened to someone wiser than myself.

The power of play is dynamic. I don't think we can overestimate the great need for maintaining this practice. When I consider my children's younger years, I am thankful we were able to homeschool—for this choice gave my children the freedom to play Legos for hours, build forts, play American Girl Dolls, pour over interesting picture books, take long nature walks, visit museums, and enjoy one another's company. This may not be the mode of education for your family, but finding free time somewhere in your child's schedule is essential to the emotional health and well-being of both parent and child. Peg Tyre of *Newsweek* writes:

> In the last decade, the earliest years of schooling have become less like a trip to "Mister Rogers Neighborhood" and more like SAT prep. Thirty years ago, first grade was for learning how to read. Now, reading lessons start in kindergarten and kids who don't crack the code by the middle of the first grade get extra help. Instead of story time, finger painting, tracing letters and snack, first graders are spending hours doing math work sheets and sounding out words in reading groups. In some places, recess, music, art and even social studies are being replaced by writing exercises and spelling quizzes. Kids as young as 6 are tested, and tested again—some every 10 days or so—to ensure they're making sufficient progress. After school, there's homework, and for some, educational videos, more workbooks and tutoring, to help give them an edge.[10]

Giving children an edge seems to be a consuming thought among younger parents. I taught first grade twenty-one years ago, and it was a very different learning environment. I am all for change, but only when change results in positive, forward

movement. My concern is that
the advancement of academic
requirements in the early years
will result in producing a generation of producers—overachieving
workaholics who don't know
how to "be." Little boys and girls
will grow up to be men and
women who don't know how to relax and enjoy life.

> "Children today have
> many wonderful oppor-
> tunities, but they need
> time to explore things
> in depth."[11]

Workaholism, affectionately known as "the respectable
addiction,"[12] is an obsession with work that is all-consuming.
Bryan Robinson, PhD, author of *Chained to the Desk*, writes:

> It prevents workaholics from maintaining healthy relation-
> ships, outside interests, or even taking measures to protect
> their health. Workaholics tend to seek high-stress jobs to keep
> the adrenaline rush going. This is true even if they don't work
> outside the home. We're seeing more women workaholics
> now because women are more visible in the workplace. But
> it's my belief that even before this trend, workaholics were
> doing this in the home. It could be in their parenting to the
> point where there is nothing else to balance their lives, no
> hobbies or fun or spirituality, because they spend all their time
> as the PTA president, running the youth sports league, and
> being a Scout leader.[13]

Oh, is Dr. Robinson right! Very often our own children
provide the answers to our plight of overdoing. I have worn
many hats in my homeschooling community, one being
"enrichment program director" for my local support group. In
addition to my own homeschooling, the position carried the
responsibility of leading, guiding, and encouraging all the families involved; answering their questions; helping and supporting the teachers of this program; fielding media inquiries;

training and supporting teachers; and managing the business aspects of the support group. Well, on the last day of this enrichment program, I learned an amazing lesson from Brooke, my younger daughter, who was nine at the time.

Her class was having an end-of-the-year party and she was very excited. Many times that morning, she had reminded me of the party and stressed how much she wanted me there.

"Of course, there is nowhere else I would rather be," I responded.

After teaching chapel, I was off to administer the final exam in my senior high literature course. Suddenly, I looked at my watch and realized I needed to get to the party. En route, several parents stopped me to discuss issues, so my progress was hindered! Trying not to be rude, I listened, all the while knowing I was missing the party. Finally, I broke away and arrived to find the party coming to a close. Obviously, my daughter was disappointed, but I thought she was overcoming it quite well. Little did I know.

Later that same day, she was bitten by a tick, suffered an allergic reaction, and endured huge welts and hives as a result of the bite. It was an extremely difficult situation. As I was tucking her into bed, about to say our prayers, I felt uneasy. I knew I needed to discuss the party issue and resolve any hurt that might be lodged in her little heart.

"Brooke," I asked, "why was it so important for Mommy to be at your party? Was it because all the other mommies were there?"

Hesitating for a moment, she finally spoke through her tears. "No, I just wanted you there."

I explained the events of the day and apologized. She continued, "Momma, we just don't have fun anymore. I want to have fun like we used to have. You're always running to the copy store or sitting at your computer. You're always working on something. I want to go places and play games together like we used to."

Ouch! Her words pierced my heart and spoke loud and clear, forcing me to take a good, long look in the mirror. Here was a little girl asking her mom to stop doing and start being. Even though she enjoyed this enrichment program, she missed her undistracted mother and our times of creative learning and exploration.

My tendency to overwork had gotten out of hand—again. Needless to say, after much thought, prayer, and family discussion, I didn't continue as director. My family needed me. My children needed a fully engaged mother. We made many positive changes and began having fun again. This situation was an impetus for me to evaluate. The culmination of my introspection became known as "Family Fun: The Mathematics of Family Fitness." Are you ready to see how your family is doing? Ready for a little introspection? Use this as a checklist to help move your family forward.

Family Fun: The Mathematics of Mental Fitness

1. *Add a daily diet of reading aloud. Subtract time spent in front of the television.*

The greatest memories I have are those of reading great classics together with my children. *Little House on the Prairie.* Homer Price. Beatrix Potter. Nestled on the couch, children tucked on each side, we would enter worlds unknown and meet great characters from all over the world. As American Essayist Horace Scudder (1838–1902) writes, "It may fairly be asked how we shall persuade children to read classic literature. It is a partial answer to say, 'Read it to them yourself.' If we would only consider the subtle strengthening of ties which comes from two people reading the same book together, breathing at once its breath, and each giving the other unconsciously his interpretation of it, it would be seen how in this simple habit of reading aloud lies a power too fine for analysis, yet stronger than iron in

"Reading aloud is most helpful in cultivating mental skills. Review at each reading what has gone on in plot, character development, and setting. Literature allows us to experience many things through the development of the imagination. It allows us to go many places where we might never go. It expands the horizons of the heart and mind. It increases our awareness of time —past, present and future."[14]

welding souls together. To my thinking there is no academy on earth equal to that found in many homes of a mother reading to her child."[15] There, on our living room couch, we would discuss situations, circumstances, behaviors, relationships, conflicts, character flaws, and much more. Literature always enriches our conversations as a family.

2. *Add community service projects. Subtract a steady stream of entertainment activities.*

One doesn't have to look far to help others. Usually, the need is right outside our front doors. Local soup kitchens, food banks, crisis pregnancy centers, urban missions, and others, all vying for helping hands. Giving sacrificially of time and talents is a great way to build in our children a lifelong love of service. Balancing community service and selfless giving with fun, recreational activities provides a healthy equilibrium.

3. *Add time spent walking outside, examining and discussing God's creation. Subtract busyness and rushing—hurrying and scurrying from one place to the next.*

We have talked about rushing in great detail. It erodes the quality of life we all desire.

Stage a personal revolt against rushing. Make history happen in the life of your home.

4. *Add diversity, new experiences, and change. Subtract ingrained routine and monotony.*

Experts suggest making simple changes to habits, such as: brushing your teeth with the opposite hand; sitting in different places at the dinner table; changing your usual route in the supermarket. Order is a good thing, but ingrained routine and monotony create a stale environment. Switch it up. That's one reason I love family vacations. They stretch each family member's comfort zone—which hurts a bit—but help each remain flexible and selfless.

5. *Add learning a new word every day. Subtract educational complacency.*

Invigorate your home's academic environment by discussing topics that will both stimulate and educate. Throw a new word out at the dinner table. Maybe *loquacious, corpulent,* or *formicary.* Check out http://wordsmith.org/awad/ for fun words (like gargantuan or pretentious).

6. *Add games you play together: board games, learning games, physical games, and puzzles. Subtract video games.*

One night at the dinner table, when Grant was about eight, he asked, "Is there somewhere I can go to silly school?"

With a big grin, I said, "Sure. Clown schools teach you how to be silly."

"And I think we should tell one joke at dinner. It is important to laugh every day," he said. "And can we make Friday nights game night?"

God gave us a son who thoroughly enjoys life. Grant is the one who continues to bring us together around a board game. It doesn't matter what the game is—it could be Clue, Monopoly, or Life. Within minutes, we discover things about each other that we had no idea even existed!

7. *Add stimulating experiences, such as family vacations and field trips. Subtract feeling confined to traditional models of learning.*

My husband and I found the greatest way to foster family unity was to make family vacations a high priority. We love to travel. Neither of us had the opportunity as children to take regular family vacations, so we decided early on to budget for family trips. Time away from the normal routine provides a great environment for family growth. One particular vacation left a big impression on our family.

Having saved our hard-earned money all year for a week of solace and sunshine in Avon, North Carolina, we were looking forward to our time at the beach. I reserved a nice cottage via the Internet from a reputable real estate company. Upon arrival, we saw that our cottage wasn't everything it was proclaimed to be. Aghast, we proceeded to unpack the car and work on having a positive attitude. We settled in and tried to overlook the inadequacies of our home away from home. But, several days into our vacation, we became infested, one by one, with very large, Saw Palmetto cockroaches (native to the Outer Banks of North Carolina). We continued to press on, but finally, after a huge downpour and a Terminix® Pest Control visit, they came marching into our cottage in full force. Extremely tense, Rob prayed. We all prayed.

Trying to keep it all in perspective, we pressed on, but no one wanted to go to bed. No one wanted to unzip a suitcase or eat (as you can imagine). So, after much convincing that everything would be fine, I wished all three children a good night. I was surprised to hear all three of them ask the same question:

"What is Daddy going to do?"

All I could say was, "Trust Daddy. He knows what to do and he will handle it."

Before going to bed, I wrote in my journal, "Okay, God. I am going to trust you in this. You have taught me how to trust. This is a big test, but by faith I am going to trust you. You know what to do and you will handle it." The next morning, I awoke early and went for a prayer walk on the beach. I was praying fervently for Rob. When I returned, he said, "We're going to the real estate office. Both of us."

The manager offered to send the Terminix people again. Rob declined that offer. She said she would find us another cottage. They couldn't find one in our price range. "We only have big beachfront rentals," she reported.

"That would be fine," Rob told her (for the same cost, of course).

She didn't like that idea. Rob took a deep breath and asked for a complete refund. They complied. We were absolutely astounded. We honestly weren't expecting a full refund. We walked out relieved, but were faced with a big decision.

"What do we do now? Where do we go? Do we go home? This is our only vacation time. Lord, help us," we prayed. "Show us what in the world to do next."

Rob said, "Let's check out this place I saw on the way in . . . Avon Cottages."

We did. We shared our woes with the manager and he handed us five or six keys to cottages twice the size of our original cottage—some beachfront, some a short walk from the beach, fully loaded, beautiful, and clean—that he had available and would rent to us on a daily basis. Unbelievable!

> "Trust Daddy" is now a beloved principle that we hold closely.

We rented #82. God had moved on our behalf. The looks on the children's faces were priceless. They ran around the new cottage with such joy and celebration, and saw that they could trust Daddy (and so could I)—he does care.

It may sound simple, but within these life lessons we discover the spiritual fabric of our family. Children watch, more than we would like at times, how we handle people, problems, and pernicious situations. Remember, stone by stone—lesson by lesson—a family becomes rock-solid. God has an incredible way of taking devastation and transforming it into something beautiful and delightful. The journey is arduous, but necessary.

We also loved to encourage natural curiosity in our children by taking field trips—lots of little adventures to parks, local museums, the beach, or a forest, or a walk around the neighborhood. The simplest, yet most rewarding, were our day trips to the Outer Banks of North Carolina. Fortunate to live near the ocean, the beach always offered a plethora of experiences—building sand castles and cities, finding whirlpools of water full of shells and sea life, and plenty of good food and sunshine.

8. *Add invigorating conversation around the dinner table. Subtract a habit of eating on the run or in front of the television.*

There is definitely a problem when America feels the need to organize a "National Family Night" in order to encourage Americans to set aside one night a year for family time, a time without scheduled activities. Dr. Alvin Rosenfeld, a leading expert on overscheduled children, hopes this national event will awaken parents to the need to slow down the pace of their lives.

Miriam Weinstein writes, "Family supper is one more quaint artifact, like vinyl records or manual typewriters. Dinner is held hostage to the all important schedule, with little time or opportunity to talk."[16]

You might ask, "How could sitting around the dinner table make such a difference?" I used to wonder about that myself. But, after twenty years of sitting around the dinner table with our three children, I can vouch for the huge difference it makes. Magical things happen around the dinner table, between passing the salt and asking someone to refill the water pitcher. Ideas are shared. Jokes are told. Manners are taught. World affairs are discussed. Problems are solved. Politics is debated. National tragedies are mourned. Bonds that are deep and holy are formed.

Dinnertime is the one family ritual I will deeply miss. I remember the first meal we shared after our oldest went to college. It was a solemn event. Her chair was empty. Her voice was